MW00605399

# Navigating Your Federal Retirement Benefits

## Strategies, Tips, and Best Kept Secrets

### John F. Stohlman

**MS, CFP®, CLU®, ChFC®, ChFEBC℠, CEP®**

### &

### Laura S. Stohlman

**CFP®, ChFEBC℠, CEP®, RFC®**

Copyright © 2014 by John F. Stohlman & Laura S. Stohlman
All rights reserved

Navigating Your Federal Retirement Benefits:
Strategies, Tips, and Best Kept Secrets

All rights reserved. No part of this publication may be reproduced, stored in a retrieval system or transmitted in any form or by any means – for example, electronic, mechanical, photocopy, scanning, recording or otherwise - except as permitted under code 107 or 108 of the 1976 United States Copyright Act, without the prior written permission of the authors. The only exception is brief quotations in printed reviews.

ISBN 978-1-938911-54-5

Printed in the United States of America
by Total Printing Systems

Cover Design by Michael Cartwright

# DEDICATION

We dedicate this book to those who came before us, believed in us, and encouraged us to do and be the best we could be.

**Our parents**:

Tom & Edna Searles

Joyce D. Stohlman

**In memory of**:

John (Jack) Stohlman, Sr.

C. Elizabeth Stohlman

Eugene (Poppa) & Mary Louise (Momma) Searles

Prentiss (Poppa) W. Lowe

## One of our favorite quotes:

*"If you don't know where you are going, you'll end up someplace else."*

~ Yogi Berra

# ACKNOWLEDGEMENTS

We would like to give special thanks to:

Dan & Eydie Searles, whom we are pleased to call both family and business partners. They have contributed to our lives much more than can ever be measured.

Ryan Dunn, our newest business partner, whose excitement and enthusiasm has and continues to rub off on us.

Our staff at both Federal Navigators and Medallion Financial Group. It is a privilege to work with this group of outstanding people. Much appreciation goes to Marie Michur and Natalie Waibel, for editing and re-editing and all the others who had a hand in the process.

Malcolm Munro, who passed on his knowledge of publishing and his encouragement to "just get started and write it."

Our current clients. We are honored that you believe in us and allow us to help you navigate and map out your road to retirement. To those who are government employees, we thank you for allowing us to help you on your journey through the maze of government rules and regulations.

# GOALS OF THIS BOOK

- To be a starting point in your journey to plan your exit strategy and to ultimately achieve your retirement goals

- To help you develop an understanding of your core federal benefits and how they relate to your retirement

- To describe the basic retirement planning techniques

- To highlight important ideas and aspects of your federal benefits

- To help you avoid pitfalls and poor election choices

- To give you a working handbook to guide you with your benefits choices

- To provide a list of important contacts for additional information as needed

*"Not planning for retirement may be hazardous to your wealth."*

~ Anonymous

# TABLE OF CONTENTS

Introduction

# INTRODUCTION

As you are probably already aware, retirement for Federal Employees is a very complex system of benefit elections and choices that must be negotiated. If and when you combine these choices with other factors such as Social Security, taxes, and investing, the complexity multiplies. In fact, we have spoken to some employees who say it can feel a bit overwhelming.

As Financial Advisors, we have been helping Federal Employees with their retirement planning for over 27 years, and we agree that you have one of the most complicated benefit systems around. We also think that it is one of the <u>best</u>. However, you must learn to navigate the many rules, regulations, and unique twists and turns to leverage these benefits wisely.

Our goal in writing this book is to act as your guide, pointing out opportunities and pitfalls; thus bringing to light some little-known and misunderstood features so you can make the most of your extensive benefits. If successful, we will help you navigate your way safely to retirement so that you know what to expect along the way.

*"We are all inventors, each sailing out on a chart, of which there is no duplicate. The world is all gates, all opportunities."*

~ Ralph Waldo Emerson

***John & Laura's Tip:*** We suggest you jot down the items specific to your situation, along with page numbers, for easy reference.

**YOUR NOTES:**

# CHAPTER 1

## WHAT'S SO SPECIAL ABOUT RETIREMENT PLANNING FOR FEDERAL EMPLOYEES?

The complexity of the federal benefits system can give you the feeling of being in a very complex maze and as Federal Employee you may already realize this. What you may not know is that it is one of the best benefit systems left.

Why do we say that? We have been working with both Federal Employees and those in the private sector for over 27 years. Over these many years of assisting both private and civil servants through the entire retirement process, we have had the opportunity to compare and contrast the planning needs and benefits of both groups. The first point that comes to mind when comparing the two groups is that for retirement planning, the Federal Employee has unique needs because of the intricacy of the benefit systems. The second point is that if the Federal Employee can learn how to navigate the many rules, regulations and unique twists and turns, then they will also have a collection of superior employee benefits when compared to most non-Federal Employees.

First, let's talk about the complexity of the Federal Employee retirement and benefits system.

As a Federal Employee:

1. You have two substantially different retirement systems depending on when you started employment with the Federal Government: The Civil Service Retirement System (CSRS, the old system) and the Federal Employee Retirement System (FERS, the new system). The pension

calculation, benefit opportunities, and retirement eligibility all differ from each other. The retirement software or Financial Advisor you choose to guide you must understand the nature and calculations of your system, or mistakes will be made. Even worse, you may lose out on opportunities for yourself, your spouse, or your heirs.

2. You have a defined benefit pension. Whether you are "old system" CSRS or "new system" FERS, if you work long enough you will have a pension. Simply having a pension is better than most private sector employees. Most companies have long done away with pensions and replaced them with 401(k)s, with some employers matching employee contributions and some not. While these are good retirement savings vehicles, the income they provide does not compare to the guarantees provided with a pension. With your CSRS or FERS pension you have the most reliable source of income in retirement – the U.S. Government. Yet another degree of separation between your pension and those few remaining in private industry is the COLA (Cost Of Living Adjustment), which can augment your government pension income when you retire. This is a huge bonus that most non-government pensions do not offer.

3. There are a lot of forms and benefit elections to select as you enter retirement and it is up to you to read and understand your options and to properly complete them. Elections must be made on time, in good order, and you want

to make sure that you have not made a mistake or missed any opportunities because you did not understand the forms. Mistakes can potentially delay your pension income and can even negate specific benefits altogether.

4. The government provides pre-retirement classes in abundance. However, these classes are designed to educate groups and often leave out information on how to apply your benefits to your specific situation. The instructors of the classes are often unable to take the time necessary to incorporate your individual "Big Picture" into your benefit elections. For example, how does Social Security for you and your spouse (or future spouse) integrate with your pension(s) when you retire? This can be very involved. In addition, how Social Security integrates with CSRS and FERS pensions is entirely different.

5. In addition to being non-specific to your situation, these classes are extremely complex and often cover several confusing topics in one session. Our clients have stated that they, "missed much of the information due to information overload." This is why we believe this book is needed. As we like to say, "So you can eat the elephant one bite at a time."

## Thrift Savings Plan (TSP)

The TSP can be a wonderful tool to help accumulate savings in preparation for retirement. However, it has serious limitations when it comes to distribution or income options at retirement. For example: 1) limited flexibility as far as diversification; 2) rigid rules regarding access to your funds; and 3) confusing distribution options that require special attention so you don't unintentionally disinherit your spouse or children/heirs. We will address these topics in greater depth in future chapters.

## Keeping Your Health Insurance (FEHBP) in Retirement

As a qualified Federal Employee, the option to continue your health insurance into retirement is a rare benefit. Even better, the government pays just over 70% of the premium cost for you! Although some private-sector employees are allowed to maintain their health insurance benefits into retirement, we have never encountered a private company that pays the majority of the costs.

## Your Benefits Might Allow for an Earlier Retirement

*FERS only*: FERS employees have a special benefit called the "FERS Supplement" that integrates with Social Security benefits for immediate retirement once you have met your MRA (minimum retirement age). This benefit can cause your Federal Retirement income to start, and change in ways that can confuse standard retirement software and many Financial

Advisors as well. This is another example of why we believe this book is important. We hope that it will help you become more informed about all of your benefit options, so you can make good decisions as you plan for and enter retirement. We will cover the FERS Supplement in greater depth in Chapter 10.

*CSRS only*: You may be eligible for a benefit that is not available to FERS employees, nor is it provided to any private-sector employee. It is called the Voluntary Contribution Program or VCP. Generally speaking, the VCP allows you to invest up to 10% of your aggregated career earnings into the account. This account can then be used as 1) a tax-deferred savings account; 2) another annuity at retirement; or 3) a source of funds that may be converted to a Roth IRA that has special tax benefits for the remainder of your life! We will discuss the features of the VCP in greater depth later. Again, this is a unique benefit just for CSRS employees.

We have only begun to describe the assortment of unique yet complex benefits that are offered only to Federal Employees. This is what makes their retirement planning special. We feel that it is also one of the best collections of benefits. If you learn to navigate all the forms, rules, regulations, elections, and options involved in proper planning, these benefits may allow you to get a head start on an earlier retirement than many others in the private sector.

It is very important to understand that when planning for retirement, your federal benefits are only one piece of the financial puzzle. Every person has a unique story, life situation, and financial needs.

Your federal benefits should be integrated into your "Big Financial Picture," so that all the areas of your financial life are connected:

Retirement Plan / Distribution (Income)

Estate Plan / Beneficiaries

Tax Plan / Income Taxes Where and When You Retire

Life Insurance Plan / FEGLI

Investment Plan / Selections on TSP / IRA

The selections / elections you make in one plan can affect the other areas in a positive or negative manner. Also, you need to realize that the decisions you make regarding your pension, life insurance and other benefit options can also affect the retirement and financial plans of your spouse and other dependents significantly.

Many Financial Advisors may not thoroughly understand the federal benefit systems. What makes sense for "most people" may not be what is best for you as a Federal Employee, *because you are unique and different.* Overall, that's a good thing!

# Comprehensive Retirement Strategy for Federal Employees

**Our Holistic Approach for a Successful Retirement**

We recommend using a Holistic Approach to help you develop and implement a complete program designed specifically to your unique family situation, so that you have a successful retirement.

*"A good financial plan is a road map that shows us exactly how the choices we make today will affect our future."*

~ Alexa Von Tobel

# CHAPTER 2

## ESTIMATING YOUR RETIREMENT INCOME AND EXPENSES (MAKING A REAL BUDGET)

> *"A goal without a plan is just a wish."*
>
> ~ Antoine de Saint-Exupery

One of the greatest fears of Federal Employees as they enter retirement is the possibility of running out of money. Proper retirement planning is one of the best tools available to attempt to lower the chance of that eventuality. We have been aiding Federal Employees with their retirement planning for over 25 years, which sometimes starts with a discussion about the best way to make and use a budget.

One question we discuss with pre-retirees is whether they have enough income and assets to retire **and stay** comfortably retired for life. Did you pay attention to the last part of the prior sentence, "and stay comfortably retired for life?" This alters the calculations a bit doesn't it? This means you cannot just look forward to the next couple of years, or even ten. We are talking about the remainder of your life! If your money stops working for you, you will have to go back to work or rely on your children. Unfortunately, on occasion we have had to advise a client, "After looking at the data, you can't afford to retire yet." This information is rarely taken well and understandably so. Often, we can help determine if the problem can be resolved by: 1) reducing projected retirement expenses; 2) postponing retirement for a few years; 3) working part-time during retirement; or 4) saving more in the last few years before retirement. Sometimes pre-retirees can "buy-down" their current residence or move to a state that has cheaper homes or lower taxes. Some states treat Social Security and federal pensions in a more tax-favorable way. Regardless of how the shortfall is addressed, the first step is to discover it.

## How Do You Determine if You Have a Retirement Income Shortfall?

Several methods are available to estimate the amount of income you will need once you retire. Some Advisors will use rule-of-thumb estimates such as 70% of your current income. For example, if your pre-retirement income is $100,000 a year, you can expect to need $70,000 annually in retirement. This type of estimation can be dangerous and ignores specifics that can increase or decrease your income needs.

A more comprehensive method involves looking at the changes to your expenses after retirement. On the next page, we have provided a simplified example for informational purposes.

## Retirement Income Calculation

| | |
|---|---|
| **Income While Working** | $120,000 |

**Subtractions**

| | |
|---|---|
| Lower Income Taxes | - $ 7,290 |
| No FICA Social Security/Medicare Tax | -   6,000 |
| No More Saving For Retirement | - 10,000 |
| Lower Housing Cost (mortgage paid) | -   6,000 |
| Lower Expenses (no commute/work clothes) | -   1,000 |
| **Total** | ($30,290) |

**Additions**

| | |
|---|---|
| Higher Health Care Cost | 5,000 |
| Travel Budget | 6,000 |
| **Total** | $11,000 |

| | |
|---|---|
| **Income Needed in Retirement** | $100,710 |

Your projection should address important topics such as:

1. Paying off your mortgage.

2. Whether you plan to live in the same home or buy-down to a smaller home.

3. Will you travel? How much?

4. Did you factor in medical costs?

5. Will your insurance costs increase?

6. Did you factor in inflation?

7. What about federal, state and local taxes? It is my experience that this is the most frequently underestimated expense when figuring out retirement income expenses.

## How Might Inflation Impact Your Retirement?

When designing your retirement plan and investment portfolio, it is important to invest with inflation in mind. Inflation decreases your purchasing power over time and erodes investment returns. To maintain your standard of living over a retirement that could last 25 to 30 years or more, you must combat the erosive effect of inflation.

The average rate of inflation for the last 30 years was 2.82%*. A $25,000 annual pension income in 1984 would only have the purchasing power of $10,854 in 2014. This works out to a loss of over 56.5% of the original purchasing power over 30 years.

Let's look at another example: if you retire in 2015 needing $50,000 per year to cover expenses, you would need $66,000 in 2025 and over $87,200 in 2035 just to maintain the same purchasing power. This is assuming the average rate of inflation does not increase above 2.82%.

*Source: US Department of Labor. December 1984 through December 2014

# How Long Should You Project You Will Live in Retirement?

When we compile a retirement projection, we routinely run the hypothetical illustration numbers to age 100, because people are living longer as a result of medical and nutritional advances. Your life expectancy could be much longer than you anticipate. In fact, married couples age 62 have a joint life expectancy of nearly 30 years, according to government tables.

## Life Expectancy Table*

| AGE | FEMALE | MALE | JOINT** |
|-----|--------|------|---------|
| 60 | 24.3 | 21.3 | 30.9 |
| 61 | 23.5 | 20.5 | 29.9 |
| 62 | 22.6 | 19.7 | 29.0 |
| 63 | 21.8 | 19.0 | 28.1 |
| 64 | 21.0 | 18.2 | 27.1 |
| 65 | 20.2 | 17.5 | 26.2 |
| 66 | 19.4 | 16.8 | 25.3 |
| 67 | 18.6 | 16.1 | 24.4 |
| 68 | 17.8 | 15.4 | 23.5 |
| 69 | 17.1 | 14.7 | 22.6 |
| 70 | 16.3 | 14.0 | 21.8 |
| 71 | 15.6 | 13.4 | 20.9 |
| 72 | 14.9 | 12.7 | 20.0 |
| 73 | 14.2 | 12.1 | 19.2 |
| 74 | 13.5 | 11.5 | 18.4 |
| 75 | 12.8 | 10.9 | 17.6 |

*Source: IRS PUB No. 590 (2012).
**At least one spouse is expected to live this long.

As Financial Advisors we are <u>less</u> worried about the first few years of retirement and <u>more</u> concerned about 25 or 30 years in the future. We believe it is important for pre-retirees to generate hypothetical retirement income illustrations to help reduce the risk of running out of money resulting from underestimating how long they might live.

> *"If I'd only known I was going to live this long, I would have taken better care of myself."*
>
> ~ Eubie Blank (died at 96)

## The Typical Spending Life Cycle

### Phase One (The "Go-Go" Years):

When we are discussing retirement expenses with our clients, we remind them that many retirees follow an expense pattern that can best be described as predictable. Very often the first 10 years of retirement tend to be the "Go-Go" spending years. New retirees tend to travel more, visit grandchildren, work part-time and begin new hobbies. If a client is going to buy-down their home and relocate, this will typically occur during the first 10 years of retirement. There are many reasons for this spending burst in the first few years, but we think it's simply due to having more energy and fewer health concerns.

**Phase Two (The "Go-Slow" Years):**

The second 10 years of retirement tend to have a slower spending pace than the first 10 years. This "Go-Slow" trend will normally play out with fewer trips, more time at home, and less energy for newer projects or lifestyle changes. Many people who enter this phase will no longer work part-time. They may find that travel expenses are replaced with more doctor visits and home modifications. The pace is just a bit slower during phase two.

**Phase Three (The "No-Go" Years):**

The third and final phase of the retirement spending cycle is the later "No-Go" years. In this period of the spending cycle people have much less energy and capacity for new projects. They travel much less and are often visited rather than visit. They are definitely in maintenance mode, and do not want to move to new residences unless required to because of failing health. They typically do not like change in this phase. During this time of life they can experience higher medical and/or nursing care costs.

We all know that not everyone fits into this three-phase pattern. Some people have more energy and resources to continue a faster pace for a longer period of time. On the other hand, it is not unusual for a health event to force someone into the "No-Go" period just a few years into retirement.

Knowing that spending patterns change throughout retirement, we believe it is helpful to know that these changes often have a predictable pattern. The real question is, "What will your spending cycle look like?" This should be considered in your projections.

> *"A nickel ain't worth a dime*
>
> *anymore."*
>
> ~ Yogi Berra

# CHAPTER 3

## THRIFT SAVINGS PLAN (TSP) BASICS

The TSP is a defined contribution plan, which simply means the employee is permitted to define how they will deposit money into the plan. These contributions are generally made pre-tax. In private industry this type of arrangement is called a 401(k), and in a nonprofit organization, a 403(b).

The TSP is a retirement savings plan for Federal Employees. All Federal Employees may participate and are encouraged to do so. All the systems (CSRS, CSRS Offset, and FERS) may participate upon their employment.

The Thrift Savings Plan provides numerous advantages including:

- Automatic payroll deductions

- A number of investment options including lifecycle funds

- A choice of Traditional (pre-tax) TSP or Roth (post-tax) TSP

- Low administrative and management fees

# Investing in the TSP

The TSP offers two approaches to investing your money:

1. **The L Funds** - Better known as the Lifecycle funds, L funds are invested according to professionally designed allocations of the five standard funds (C, F, G, S and I), which include stocks, bonds, and government securities. You select your L Fund based on the date you plan to retire and start distributions. For example, if you are anticipating retirement in 2019 you may invest in the 2020 fund. **TIP:** It is important to understand that the L Funds investment allocation orientations are very general and may not be well-suited for you or your goals!

2. **Individual Funds** - These are five core funds, described below, that allow you to make your own decisions regarding your investment allocations. Using these funds, it is possible to construct a portfolio and make allocation changes at your own discretion and according to your tolerance for risk.

   **The Government Securities Investment (G) Fund** - The G Fund is invested in short-term U.S. Treasury securities. It gives you the opportunity to earn a modest interest with no risk of loss of principal. Payments of principal and interest are guaranteed by the U.S Government.

**The Fixed Income Index Investment (F) Fund** - The F Fund is invested in a bond index that tracks the Barclays Capital U.S. Aggregate Bond Index. This is a broad index representing U.S. Government, mortgage-backed, corporate, and foreign government sectors of the bond market.

**The Common Stock Index Investment (C) Fund** - The C Fund is invested in a stock index fund that tracks the Standard and Poor's 500 (S&P 500) Stock Index. This is a market index made up of 500 large-to-medium-sized U.S. companies.

**The Small Capitalization Stock Index (S) Fund** - The S Fund is invested in a stock index fund that tracks the Dow Jones U.S Completion Total Stock Index (TSM). This is a market index of small-to-medium-sized U.S Companies that are not included in the S&P 500 index.

**International Stock Index Investment (I) Fund** - The I Fund is invested in a stock index fund that tracks the Morgan Stanley Capital International EAFE (Europe, Australia, Far East) index. This is a broad international market index, made up primarily of large companies of the major developed countries.

# Contributions into the TSP

Participants are entitled to contribute a percentage of their basic salary each year up to a maximum amount, which changes every year. For 2015 it is $18,000.

Special catch-up provisions apply for employees age 50 and over. As of 2015, participants age 50 or older are permitted to add an additional amount of $6,000. This means the total amount for 2015 for those 50 and over is $24,000 ($18,000 + $6,000).

However, there are differences in the CSRS and FERS retirement systems with respect to the TSP and how it is funded. So let's discuss them:

## FERS Employees and the TSP

### Agency Automatic (1%) Contributions

If you are a FERS employee, Uncle Sam will contribute an amount equal to 1% of your basic pay each pay date to your TSP account. There is no waiting period and you need not contribute to the TSP to get it. This amount is automatically invested into the G fund, which is one of the investment options provided in the TSP. You may change this allocation whenever you wish.

This 1% is not taken from your pay nor is it added to your pay for income tax purposes.

## Vesting of the 1% Agency Contributions

There are vesting rules associated with the government's deposit to your TSP. This means you must remain employed in government service for a minimum period of time before separating from service or you may forfeit these contributions and the earnings associated with them. Currently, the minimum service requirement is three years.

## Matching Contributions

If you are a FERS employee, you will also receive Agency Matching Contributions from the government based on the amount you contribute to the TSP. CSRS employees are not eligible for these matching contributions.

As a FERS employee, the match is calculated based on the first 5% of pay you contribute each pay period. The first 3% of pay that you deposit will be matched dollar-for-dollar. The next 2% will be matched at 50 cents on each dollar for a total additional contribution of 4%. Any contributions over 5% are not matched.

It is important to know the maximum FERS match is up to 4% per year. See the following Chart for details.

Here is how it works:

| If you put in: | The government puts in: |
| --- | --- |
| Nothing | 1% (Agency Contribution) |
| 1% | 2% |
| 2% | 3% |
| 3% | 4% |
| 4% | 4.5% |
| 5% | 5% |

## Opportunity Missed

It is our professional opinion that every FERS employee should contribute <u>at least</u> 5% into the Thrift Savings Plan to capitalize on the matching contribution. Let me ask a question: Where else can you invest 5% of your salary and have an immediate 100% return the same day? That is essentially what the match allows.

If a FERS employee elects not to invest in the TSP, they are refusing an offer by the government to give them a pay raise.

If cash flow is tight and prevents you from contributing to the TSP, it's worth taking time to review your financial situation. Look for ways to restructure your budget so you can lower expenses and have the cash flow that will enable you to contribute 5% to the TSP in order to receive the maximum 4% match. Remember, you get 1% whether you contribute or not.

Today it is estimated that approximately 10% of FERS employees do not invest <u>any</u> of their own money in the TSP, thus foregoing the match altogether.

## For FERS TSP Contributions - Timing Does Matter

Contributions to the TSP may be either a specific dollar amount per paycheck or a percentage of income.

As a FERS employee it is important to note that the government match is linear and calculated each pay period throughout the year. Therefore, if you do not contribute in a given pay period you will have missed the match for that pay period.

For example, if you deposit your full annual TSP contribution of $18,000 in the first six months of the year, you will miss your match in the second half of the year because you will not be contributing. So when contributing to your TSP, timing matters! Spread out your contributions evenly over the year to cover each pay period in order to avoid missing part of your match.

## How Much Should You Contribute to Your TSP as a FERS Employee?

The simple answer to this question is, "probably more than you think." As a FERS employee, you are fully participating in Social Security and the FERS Retirement Plan. Using the analogy of a three-legged stool, the TSP is the third leg of that retirement stool, and as everyone knows, you can't sit on a three-legged stool without all of its legs.

Building up the TSP is also a way to hedge against the potential downsizing of Social Security in the future. We have all heard or read about the underfunding of Social Security. Currently, there is potential for government budget reductions that may impact salary increases and also result in RIFS or involuntary retirement in the coming years.

Investing in the TSP allows you to invest in your own future and helps you to control your own retirement destiny. What happens with government budgets and Social Security is out of your control, but what happens with the TSP is within your control.

## How Much Should You Invest in the TSP as a CSRS or a CSRS Offset Employee?

Again, we have found that the answer is the same: "More than you think." The fact is, in today's environment, federal jobs are not as secure as they once were. Although you do not get a match as a CSRS employee, you are still entitled to fully utilize the pre-tax and/or post-tax systematic investment available with the TSP.

## Roth Thrift Savings Plan

The TSP began offering a Roth option in 2012. This new feature combines the after-tax (no up-front tax deduction) option to the existing benefits of the TSP. Since April 2012, you could choose between two tax treatments for your TSP contribution, or you may even elect to do both!

1. **Traditional (Pre-tax):** You defer the taxes on your contributions and earnings until you withdraw them, in effect, deducting the contributions from current taxation now. Less Tax Now!

2. **Roth (After-Tax):** You pay taxes on your contributions now, as you make them, then all earnings and deposits are tax-free on withdrawal. Thus contributing to the Roth TSP will result in lower take-home pay, because you are paying the taxes now in exchange for tax-free distributions once you retire. Less Tax Later!

One may ask: "Why would I want to give up my tax deduction now?" The answer is your Roth savings may grow tax-free along with eventual withdrawals from the TSP. Put differently, the Roth TSP can be a source of tax-free income to you in retirement.

There are a couple of rules regarding withdrawals from the Roth TSP that you need to know:

1. You will not pay tax on the earnings as long as you take distributions after the age of 59½ **AND**

2. Distributions must not be made for at least five years after your first Roth contribution.

If you break either of these two rules, you will lose the tax advantages and pay a 10% penalty.

So, who should consider the Roth TSP (401k)? First, those who believe overall tax rates will increase significantly in the future, or want to hedge against that possibility; second, those that believe or hope to be in a higher personal tax bracket in retirement years; third, younger employees who could accumulate very large balances in the TSP over their career.

Even though contributions for FERS employees may be deposited into the Traditional TSP, the Roth TSP, or both, all agency contributions (the employer match) are deposited into your Traditional balance.

**John & Laura's Tip:** We believe that having a Roth contribution option gives you the ability to diversify the tax treatment of your retirement funds. We also believe that current income tax rates, which are at historic lows, will increase over time. Therefore, using the Roth TSP as a hedge against the possibility of higher taxes in the future, especially for young participants, makes a great deal of sense.

## Thrift Savings Plan Withdrawals

As a Federal Employee participating in the TSP you are allowed to withdraw money on the following occasions:

As a one-time opportunity you can make an in-service withdrawal, which is only allowed for employees age 59½ or older as they continue to work and add contributions to the plan.

This withdrawal can be made directly to you, making it fully taxable, OR the withdrawal can be made in the form of a Rollover or Transfer to an IRA. The latter would preserve the tax-deferred nature and avoid immediate taxation. The form **TSP 75** "Age-Based In-Service Withdrawal Request" is used in this instance.

If you are 55 or older when you retire or separate from service, you can withdraw funds without the 10% penalty tax normally imposed on early withdrawals. However, if you retire or separate before age 55 you are NOT allowed penalty-free withdrawals upon turning 55. You will need to postpone withdrawals until age 59½ or later to avoid the penalty tax. There is one exception: the 72(t) tax code distribution guidelines. We won't go into the details here, but if you are retiring between the age of 55 and 59½ and would like additional information on retirement plan withdrawals, please email us with your request. (See Appendix 1)

When you resign, retire, or are terminated, you are allowed access to the TSP funds. Remember that these funds are pre-tax and must be rolled or transferred to an IRA or another qualified account to avoid current taxation. The form **TSP-70** "Request for Full Withdrawal" is the form needed to execute this request.

You may also have access to a Partial Withdrawal from your TSP once you retire. Use form **TSP-77** "Request for Partial Withdrawal when Separated." This form may only be used once because federal rules state that you may only make a total of two withdrawals from the TSP unless you annuitize – which is not always the best option. **So you'll want to be re-**

ally careful, since you cannot use this form if you previously made a withdrawal.

When you are entering retirement, it is important to understand how to take income from the TSP using the income/distribution options and its restrictions.

## Moving from the Accumulation to Distribution Phase

Hopefully, you have been saving for retirement throughout your career and have been adding from your paycheck into the TSP. It has served an important function by helping you accumulate a retirement nest-egg. The TSP fund investment options (though too few choices in our opinion) have been adequate enough to give you both equity and bond options to choose from. Aside from deciding which fund allocations to use and how much to contribute, the accumulation phase has been systematic and somewhat routine.

Once you retire and elect to receive income, or perhaps move the TSP funds to IRA options, you must learn a new set of rules and choices. This is the distribution phase where you will have some very important decisions to make.

If you and your Advisor decide that you should keep your funds in the TSP after you retire, you will have three options to choose from. If you read Item 23 of the **TSP 70**, it shows the three withdrawal options: 1) Single Payment; 2) Life Annuity; and 3) TSP Monthly Payments. Make sure you are confident of your decision because in some cases once an option is chosen it cannot be changed.

1. **The Single Payment** is the first option to make withdrawals from your TSP, and is simply a lump sum

withdrawal. Be careful to estimate the taxes involved in this transaction, because the funds in the Traditional TSP are all pre-tax, meaning fully taxable, and the tax impact may be substantial.

2. **A Life Annuity** is the second distribution/income option. This is exactly what it sounds like, a payment for life. These lifetime payments are based on the following three choices as noted in the Annuity Election part XII of the **TSP 70** form.

> A. Single Life
>
> B. Joint Life with Spouse
>
> C. Joint Life with Non-Spouse Beneficiary

Within each of these options you can elect cash refund, or increasing payments, or 10-year certain sub-options. We will discuss these options in greater depth in Chapter 4, "TSP Annuity Options."

The annuity options are immediate annuities offered through Metropolitan Life (MetLife) Insurance Company, which has a contract with the government. This doesn't always mean they are the best choice. This is important because when using these annuity options, your TSP funds are no longer with the government and the old investment options (Lifecycle, C, F, G, S, I) you are familiar with are no longer available. You have traded the TSP funds for an annuity (the industry term is "annuitized"). Once completed, no modifications are allowed for the remainder of your life. If you need more income than the original monthly amount calculated, that is unfortunate, because you will not have access to it. You have given up control and the ability to make changes for the guarantee of lifetime income. Another issue to fully consider when committing your assets to annuity payments is the fact that very often little or nothing remains for your children or other heirs.

***John and Laura's Tip****:* All of these Immediate Annuity payment options offered with MetLife will lock in historically low interest rates for the remainder of your life. Would you like to lock in these low rates for the rest of your life? We're not sure that would be in your best interest as these Immediate Annuities have no hedge against the prospects for future inflation. With that said, there is a time and place to use an Immediate Annuity. There are many other highly-rated insurance companies out there that offer them, some offer COLAs or inflation riders and some even offer nursing home enhancements.

It is very important to have a conversation with a professional Advisor who is not only well-versed in the "Second Half of the Game" or distribution phase, but one who is also familiar with government benefits before you make a decision that cannot be changed.

3. **A TSP monthly payment option** is the third and final option to make withdrawals from your TSP. With this option you get to choose how much you want to receive monthly. It is a systematic distribution, <u>not to be confused with the previously described annuity option.</u>

With the monthly payment option, you can have TSP compute a lifetime payment for you based on general life expectancy and assumed/projected returns on your TSP investments. It is important to understand that these payments are in no way guaranteed and there is a real possibility that you may run out of money, since the calculation is based on a series of assumptions.

You may elect changes to your systematic monthly payment amount once each year. You may also switch back and forth between the life expectancy calculation and the monthly payment option. Additionally, you may also request a full payment or rollover of remaining funds at any time.

Changes in the amount of the monthly payment can only be made in December (for the following year). After that no additional fund withdrawals or changes are allowed for that year.

## Why Should You Consider Transferring All or Part of Your TSP to an IRA?

The Thrift Savings Plan is a good instrument in the accumulation phase when you are building the funds you need for retirement. The fees are very low, you have both equity-based and bond-based investment choices, and most importantly, it allows you to save systematically - without thinking about it over your career. Remember, as you approach and enter retirement you are moving from the accumulation phase of your life to the distribution phase of your life, or as we sometimes call it the "Second Half of the Game."

In the second half, all the rules and goals change. In this distribution phase you are more interested in producing income and less interested in growing the assets, although we believe some growth is always needed for inflation protection. So now you should think about the tax that this income will produce. In the accumulation phase there was no income tax planning because everything was tax-deferred. In the distribution phase most people are very interested in protecting the nest-egg because it is difficult (if not impossible) to go back to work and re-grow the assets over again. Often, people consider options that can provide a lifetime guarantee of income. (Remember our previous discussion?) However, we have found over our many years that they do not want to give up control or disinherit their heirs. Since the TSP has very limited withdrawal and transfer options, it is a much better accumulation vehicle than a distribution vehicle, in our view.

# The FERS Three-Legged Stool

If you are a FERS employee you are probably aware that your retirement income is structured like a three-legged stool with these components:

1. FERS Pension

2. Social Security

3. Thrift Savings Plan

How these three pieces fit together is very important. If you would like assistance in the preparation of a hypothetical illustration of the three components of your retirement, we may be able to help you. Please contact us for additional information.

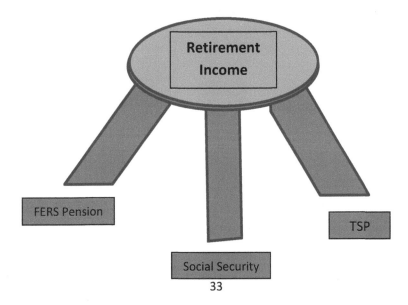

*"A good plan implemented today is better than a perfect plan implemented tomorrow."*

~ George Patton

# CHAPTER 4

## THRIFT SAVINGS PLAN ANNUITY OPTIONS

Through its provider, MetLife, the TSP offers two primary life annuity options to its participants. These can be elected in section XII, page 6 of the **TSP-70**.

1. Single Life annuity

2. Joint Life annuity with spouse/with someone other than your spouse.

Single Life Annuity: The Single Life option is designed to give you a level monthly income for as long as you live. This option provides the largest monthly check, but all payments will stop upon your death. Once you purchase this option, there is no longer any principal value remaining for your heirs. You have bought a lifetime income stream based only on your own individual life.

Joint Life Annuity: The Joint Life option will provide a monthly income to you and the person you have chosen to share the annuity with, either a spouse or non-spouse. If either one of you dies, the income will still be paid to the survivor for their lifetime.

Often, a spouse is the joint annuitant. However, you may choose a former spouse, or anyone who has an insurable interest in you. In other words, someone that stands to have a financial loss upon your death.

There are two joint options available:

100% Survivor Joint Annuity: With this option, the income stays level to the survivor regardless of which person passes first. However, the overall payments will be a lesser amount than the Single Life annuity choice.

50% Survivor Joint Annuity: With this option, if either party passes, whether it is the annuitant or the survivor, the income reduces to half. It is important to note that this rule goes both ways. **The primary annuitant's income will also be reduced to half if the spouse or joint owner dies!** This can easily be misunderstood, and has confused many who have elected it because it is very different from the way survivorship works with most other annuity companies.

### Additional Annuity Payment Features/Options

If you elect either the Single Life or Joint Life payments you will also need to choose either the Level Payment or Increasing Payment option.

Level: If you elect a Level Payment option, the payout will be higher but will remain the same for the duration of the lifetime payout.

Increasing: With this option, your payment will be adjusted annually by the amount of inflation, up to 3% per year, but will begin with less than the Level Payment option.

*John and Laura's Tip*: The increasing option has the potential to adjust for inflation over time, which is good. However, your initial payment base begins substantially lower than the level option. We feel it is best to consult with someone who is familiar with all your options, and to examine them thoroughly before making your final decision.

## Providing for Beneficiaries

You will have two additional options available to you if you choose a TSP annuity. The purpose of these options is to provide some type of payment or residual amount for heirs after the primary annuitant(s) pass away. Either of these will reduce the payment base of your annuities, resulting in a lower monthly benefit to you.

### Cash Refund:
This option will result in your beneficiary receiving the residual lump sum amount of your original TSP balance that was not paid out to you and/or your joint annuitant as income prior to death. This option will reduce your monthly benefit because you are adding a guarantee for your beneficiary.

### Ten-Year Certain:
This option is designed to ensure that either you or your beneficiaries will receive income payments from the annuity policy for at least ten years from the start date of the income. This will also reduce your life annuity because it adds a ten-

year guarantee of income payments to someone whether it is you or your beneficiary, increasing the risk to the insurance company.

***John and Laura's Tip:*** For specific annuity questions you can call the TSP-Office of Personnel Management toll free at 1-877-968-3778. For hearing impaired participants call the TDD line 1-877-847-4385. If you are living internationally call direct at 404-233-4400.

# CHAPTER 5

## REQUIRED MINIMUM DISTRIBUTIONS (RMDs)

Once you reach age 70½, the government mandates that you begin to take at least a minimum amount from your qualified funds (IRA, 401(k), 403(b), TSP) so that they can be taxed. Substantial penalties of up to 50% will apply if you are non-compliant. Your first RMD must be taken by April 1$^{st}$ of the year following the year in which you turn 70½. The following year's distribution must be taken by December 31$^{st}$. So, you may end up taking two years distributions in the first year if you are not careful. Your RMD may be taken from a single IRA or from any combination if you own more than one IRA. The amount of the distribution is determined by dividing the year-end IRA balance(s) of the preceding year by the IRS life expectancy factor. These factors are available in IRS PUB No. 590.

As a person gets older, the Required Minimum Distribution increases because of the declining life expectancy.

### Required Distribution Withdrawal Rates Summary*

| AGE | WITHDRAWAL RATES |
|-----|------------------|
| 70½ | 3.6% |
| 75 | 4.4% |
| 80 | 5.4% |
| 85 | 6.8% |
| 90 | 8.8% |

However, if your spouse is the sole beneficiary and is more than 10 years younger than you, the RMD rate will be lower.

*Source: IRS PUB No. 590, Section III

*__John and Laura's Tip:__* As you age, the RMD percentages increase. Because these withdrawals are mandatory, even in a declining market, the IRA value could decrease substantially. This may create a risk of the account being depleted so much that there will not be enough assets to last your entire life (or the life of your spouse). This is one reason why we believe holistic planning is so important.

You may need to consider strategies that can provide retirement income that will last two lifetimes. Talk to your financial professional to review your options, or contact our office. This may help you be more prepared for your retirement journey.


## Special RMD Rules for the Thrift Savings Plan

As we have already explained, once you reach age 70½, the government mandates that you begin to take at least a minimum amount from your qualified funds (IRA, 401(k), 403(b), TSP) so that they may be taxed. *__However, if you are still a government employee at this age, you need not begin mandatory withdrawals from the TSP until after you retire.__* But please note that even if you are working, if you own other IRAs, 401(k)s, or other non-government investments, you must begin your distributions on those vehicles.

This makes RMD planning a challenge with the TSP for several reasons:

First, the TSP does not assist you in the coordination of Required Minimum Distributions and calculations with other

IRAs you may have outside the TSP, so you must do this yourself.

Second, there is a very important deadline for withdrawing your TSP account. To quote the TSP, "By April 1<sup>st</sup> of the year following the year you become age 70½ and are separated from Federal service, the TSP requires that you withdraw your entire account balance in a single payment, begin receiving monthly payments, purchase a TSP annuity, or use a combination of these withdrawal options. <u>If you do not withdraw your account by the required deadline, your account balance will be forfeited to the TSP. You can reclaim your account, but you will not receive earnings on your account from the time the account was forfeited.</u> In order to reclaim your account, you must make a full withdrawal election." Please request **TSP-775**, "Important Tax Information About Your TSP Withdrawal and Required Minimum Distributions" for a full discussion.

***John and Laura's Tip***: The TSP rules are more rigid than those of an IRA. With an IRA, you have much more control and the flexibility to coordinate your RMDs.

For example, if you have three IRA accounts, you have the option to do a single large RMD withdrawal from one of your IRA accounts that will satisfy the requirement for all three of the accounts. However, if you have a TSP account after retirement, you must take annual disbursements from the TSP to satisfy the TSP requirements as described above.

## The TSP is a Self-Managed Vehicle

As you know, the management, allocation, and distribution of the TSP is up to you as the owner. We sometimes refer to it as a "Yo-Yo" account – this stands for **Y**ou're **O**n **Y**our **O**wn. The TSP is not able to provide specific investment advice, nor can it offer tax or legal advice. You simply don't have an Advisor with your TSP. As you transition to the new distribution phase of your life with a whole new set of goals and rules, doesn't it make sense to get some assistance?

***John and Laura's Tip***: Unless you are truly willing to put in the time to study and understand the structure and risks associated with investing your life's savings, it would be advisable to seek out competent counsel regarding investing and the taxation of disbursements.

## Special Estate Planning Issue and the TSP

We have been asked, "What will happen to my TSP money after I am gone?" This is an important question. One of the limitations of the TSP is its inability to transfer assets to children after the death of the participant and spouse. Tax notice TSP-583 dated May, 2012, states, "Death benefits paid from a beneficiary participant account cannot be transferred into an inherited IRA. Instead, the payment will be made directly to the beneficiary of the beneficiary participant account."

This means that after you and your spouse are deceased, your children will get a check and be responsible for paying all of the taxes associated with the distribution at that time. They are not given the opportunity to create an IRA and keep the assets tax-deferred.

## *John and Laura's Tips:*

***Tip One:*** We believe this is a serious estate planning limitation and yet another reason to move assets from the TSP to an IRA after you reach the distribution phase (retirement). Once the assets are in an IRA, moving them to an inherited IRA for the children is not an issue.

***Tip Two:*** It is also our belief that the TSP is better designed for the accumulation phase, and is less effective in managing the retiring employee's needs in the distribution phase or "Second Half of the Game." Those distribution needs are better managed in an IRA because of the greater flexibility. The following chart is a summary of the important issues in each phase.

| | Accumulation Phase (Pre-retirement) | Distribution Phase (Post-retirement) |
|---|---|---|
| **Primary Importance** | Growth | Income |
| **Taxes** | Deferred | Planning needed |
| **Protection of Principle** | Less important | More important |
| **RMD Planning** | Not necessary | Necessary |
| **Estate Planning** | Less important | More important |

"Are you prepared to play in the Second Half of the Game?

In Post-Retirement all the rules change."

~John Stohlman

# CHAPTER 6

## FEDERAL EMPLOYEE GROUP LIFE INSURANCE
## (FEGLI)

The federal government introduced FEGLI in 1954 to provide group term insurance to Federal Employees. As such, there is no cash value or paid-up value associated with the plan. Since then, it has evolved into the largest group life insurance plan in existence, covering over four million Federal Employees, retirees and their family members. The OPM has currently contracted with MetLife Insurance Company to provide this coverage and handle the administrative claims.

### Basic Insurance

The first component of FEGLI insurance is the Basic insurance. This is calculated by taking the Federal Employee's salary, rounding it up to the next $1,000, then adding an additional $2,000. For example: if your salary is $50,521/year, your Basic insurance would be $53,000 calculated as follows:

$51,000 ($50,521 rounded to the next $1,000)

$53,000 ($51,000 + $2,000)

Additionally, Basic coverage includes an extra benefit if you are under age 45 when you die. If you are under age 35 the amount of Basic insurance payable upon your death will be double the regular amount. Starting at age 36, the extra benefit reduces by 10 percent each year, until age 45 when there is no extra benefit.

All new Federal Employees are automatically enrolled in the Basic life insurance and the premiums are withdrawn from your paycheck unless you waive the coverage. The cost of Basic insurance is shared between the employee and the government. The employee pays 2/3 and the government pays 1/3. Your age does not affect your Basic insurance cost.

## FEGLI Optional Insurance

In addition to the Basic, there are three forms of Optional coverage available. If an employee is enrolled in the Basic insurance, they may then add to it using the three Optional coverages. Unlike Basic, the employee pays the full cost of these coverages, enrollment is not automatic and the cost of the insurance depends on your age.

Option A – Standard

Option B – Additional

Option C – Family

**Option A (Standard insurance):** This is a small addition of $10,000 over and above the Basic insurance.

### Employee Portion of Option A Insurance Costs

| Age Group | Biweekly Premium | Monthly Premium |
|---|---|---|
| Under 35 | $0.30 | $0.65 |
| 35-39 | $0.40 | $0.87 |
| 40-44 | $0.60 | $1.30 |
| 45-49 | $0.90 | $1.95 |
| 50-54 | $1.40 | $3.03 |
| 55-59 | $2.70 | $5.85 |
| 60 and over | $6.00 | $13.00 |

**Option B (Additional insurance):** You can add multiples of your income from one to five times the annual rate of basic salary. It is typically the most expensive form of coverage, because the amount of life insurance can be much larger than the other options. The cost of Option B coverage is based on age and increases every five years. As with most forms of term insurance, the cost generally starts out to be fairly inexpensive, growing significantly over time as shown in the chart on the next page.

Many Federal Employees elect this coverage when they first start service, usually in their 20's or 30's. When enrolling for Option B coverage as a new employee, there is no underwriting qualification, which means a person cannot be declined for health issues. Because the coverage is cheap at a young age and the employee cannot be declined, many employees decide to take the large multiples of insurance. Why not? However, as time passes, the employee moves through a particular 5-year age band (often at age 50 or 55) and notices that their pay declines. The increase in life insurance Option B Additional premiums may account for the decline.

## Employee Portion of Option B Insurance Costs (2014 Rates)

| Option B Premium per $1,000 of Insurance Age Band | Biweekly Premium | Monthly Premium |
|---|---|---|
| Under 35 | $0.02 | $0.043 |
| 35-39 | $0.03 | $0.065 |
| 40-44 | $0.05 | $0.108 |
| 45-49 | $0.08 | $0.173 |
| 50-54 | $0.13 | $0.282 |
| 55-59 | $0.23 | $0.498 |
| 60-64 | $0.52 | $1.127 |
| 65-69 | $0.62 | $1.343 |
| 70-74 | $1.14 | $2.470 |
| 75-79 | $1.80 | $3.900 |
| 80 and over | $2.40 | $5.200 |

**Option C (Family insurance):** This option can be purchased in increments of $5,000 up to $25,000 for a spouse. An eligible child can be insured in increments of $2,500 up to $12,500 per child. The cost of Option C coverage is based on the age of the employee, not the age of the spouse or children.

## Life Insurance Options at Retirement

When an employee retires, they must elect how much of the Basic and Optional insurance coverage they would like to pay for and carry into retirement.

These coverages may continue into retirement **IF**:
1. Your retirement annuity begins immediately (within a month after you separate from service).

2. You were covered for the five years immediately before your annuity began.

3. You do not elect to convert your life insurance to an individual policy.

Under FERS, there is an exception to the first item above. If you separate from service after reaching MRA (minimum retirement age) and have at least 10 years of service, you are eligible for an Immediate Annuity. Therefore, under the FERS retirement eligibility rules you may elect to postpone your annuity. If you do so, your life insurance coverage will stop until the date your annuity begins. The amount of life insurance coverage will remain the same as it was when you separated, or the amount following your 65th birthday, whichever is later.

## What do Most People do with FEGLI When They Retire?

One of the decisions that most Federal Employees need to make before entering retirement is how much of the FEGLI coverage they are going to keep. Most Federal Employees choose to keep their Basic coverage with a reduction and eliminate the Optional coverage because of its escalating costs. However, this is a very subjective issue and you should always make decisions based on your specific circumstances.

## Basic Coverage Elections in Retirement

**75% Reduction:** If you elect to continue your FEGLI Basic coverage into retirement and take the 75% reduction, your Basic will begin to decrease at age 65 or your retirement, whichever is later, eventually reaching 25% of the original amount. The rate of decrease at 2% each month will take about three years to level out at 25%. The coverage amount will not decline below 25%.

This seems to be the most popular option for retiring employees, because there is no cost to the employee for the Basic coverage if this election is chosen. But in our experience we have found that it is not always the best choice.

**50% Reduction:** If you elect the 50% reduction in your Basic Life Insurance, it will begin decreasing by 1% of the original amount each month after you retire or turn 65, whichever is later. It will continue to decrease at this rate until it levels out at 50% of the original amount, normally within four or five years. This choice can be expensive and is typically not elected. If the coverage is needed, an analysis should be done to see if a more cost effective coverage could be purchased outside the FEGLI plan in the private industry before a final election is made.

## Option B Coverage Elections at Retirement

**Full Reduction:** Once you retire and reach age 65, the coverage decreases by 2% of the pre-retirement amount each month until it reaches zero in approximately four years.

**No Reduction:** The coverage remains the same and the cost of the coverage is also unchanged as it compares to an active employee. The cost for Option B Additional insurance will increase every five years until you turn 80. This will lead to substantial cost increases at ages 65, 70, 75, and 80, causing most people to opt out of this election. If they do elect to keep the coverage with no reduction they are often surprised at the cost increases at the five-year increments.

## Options to Increase FEGLI Coverage

Currently employed Federal Employees are eligible to increase their FEGLI coverage, but only with medical proof of insurability. This means the insurance company reserves the right to decline additional coverage if your health does not meet their guidelines.

Options to increase FEGLI coverage do not apply to retirees (unless they return to active status).

## When is the Next FEGLI Open Season Scheduled?

FEGLI life insurance open seasons are extremely rare and none are currently scheduled. The most recent FEGLI open season was held in 2004. Eligible employees can only enroll or increase their coverage by taking a physical exam or with a Qualifying Life Event, such as getting married.

**How to File for Federal Employee Group Life Insurance Benefits**

Should your beneficiary need to file a death claim for benefits under FEGLI, they will need to complete one of the following two forms:

**FE-6** "Claim for Death Benefits" for Basic and Option A or B (used upon the death of an employee).

**FE-6 DEP** "Statement of Claim, Option C – Family Life Insurance" (Used upon the death of a spouse or child).

If help is needed and you are a current employee, contact the human resources office. If you are retired, contact the Office of Federal Group Life insurance at 800-633-4542. Filing a death claim requires a certified copy of the death certificate and the completed form be sent to the insured's agency if he or she died while an employee. If the employee was already retired, the form and death certificate should be sent to the Office of Personnel Management, Retirement Operations Center.

**Beneficiary Changes to FEGLI Life Insurance**

You cannot make changes to your life insurance coverage online, however, you can download the form that you will need by going to www.opm.gov.

As of this printing you should click on "A-Z Index" near the top of the page. Scroll down to "Forms" and click. Then click on "Standard Forms." Next, scroll down and click on

**SF 2823**, "Designation of Beneficiary, Federal Employees Group Life Insurance Program."

### *John and Laura's Tips:*

*Tip One:* Take the government up on Basic coverage. The actual cost of the Basic coverage is shared by the government. The employee pays approximately 2/3 and the government pays 1/3 of the premium. An employee's age doesn't affect the cost of Basic as with the other Options. Basic premiums will only increase if and when you get a raise or promotion that results in a higher salary that leads to your coverage increasing.

*Tip Two:* The Optional coverage A, B and C may be less expensive with private insurance companies outside the government, but costs are greatly dependent on your health. If you or a family member are considered uninsurable or have a significant health issue, the FEGLI options may be the best choice. It is imperative that you work with a qualified life insurance representative or underwriter who can help you examine all of the options available to you within FEGLI and outside the government.

*Tip Three:* The cost of Option B is typically competitive up until age 39. As you can see by the chart on page 48, the cost starts to increase at age 40 and continues to increase every fifth year thereafter until you turn 80. By looking at the chart you can see that the cost of coverage increases tenfold or 1000% from age 39 to 60, and continues to increase well into retirement.

Those who have a significant amount of life insurance (several multiples of income) typically find that it eventually becomes too expensive to keep. If the coverage is dropped, all premiums ever paid into the policy are lost with no benefits because this coverage does not build any cash value.

***Tip Four***: If you are able to qualify for private insurance it can be used for many purposes. You can use it for family protection (income insurance) in case you die, as a retirement income supplement, or to replace all or part of the survivor's benefit of the retirement annuity. For a further discussion of this topic please refer to the Pension Income Maximization section Chapter 7.

## How Much Life Insurance Do I Need to Carry Into Retirement?

We have been working in the life insurance industry since 1986 helping Federal Employees and their families, as well as corporate officers, answer this question. We have determined that there is no single answer to this question.

There are many factors to consider regarding the amount of life insurance you may need:

1. Do you want or need additional income for family survivors?

2. Do you want or need funds to pay off debts? If so, how much?

3. Do you need funds to pay death taxes?

4. Do you want extra money to pay educational expenses of children or grandchildren?

5. Will your spouse need supplemental retirement income?

6. Is a lump sum needed at death for a survivor emergency fund?

7. Is there an ongoing income need for a spouse based on his or her ability to work?

8. Are there any one-time expenses you wish to fund? (Such as health care expenses, family weddings, car, home improvement, etc.).

9. How much do you have in liquid investments that could be used by your survivors for final expenses, living expenses, and taxes?

Perhaps your personal need for life insurance in retirement is minimal or even nothing at all. These are just some of the questions to ask when considering how much life insurance you will need in retirement.

*"Life Insurance is mis-named; it should be called "Income Replace-ment Insurance."*

*You need it if you have a spouse, child or other relative who is depend-ent on your income."*

~Laura Stohlman

# CHAPTER 7

## LIFE INSURANCE AS A SUBSTITUTE FOR SURVIVOR BENEFITS "PENSION MAX"

### Quick Review of Survivor Benefits

All Federal Employees are eligible to participate in the Federal Retirement Program, also called pension or annuity. This is the retirement income you will be eligible for based on your age and years of service at your retirement date. CSRS, CSRS Offset, and FERS all contribute to this annuity each pay period. All new Federal Employees will be in the FERS system.

In addition to providing you an income during retirement, you will be given the opportunity to provide a portion of this benefit to your spouse in the event of your early death. This benefit is often referred to as a survivor or spousal benefit. This benefit is not free, and providing this income benefit to your spouse will decrease your Single benefit option. The reductions and income amounts vary according to your system.

For a FERS employee the options are:

1. No survivor or spousal benefit. Under this option there is no cost or reduction on your Single Life annuity.

2. 25% of your Single benefit is provided to your spouse, costing you 5% of your full benefit.

3. 50% of your Single benefit to be provided to your spouse. The cost to you would be 10% of your full benefit.

For a CSRS Annuitant the options are:

1. No survivor benefit (same as described for FERS).

2. From 0% up to 55% of the full benefit or a specific dollar amount. You decide how much to provide and the government will calculate it for you. It is important to remember that if you want to provide health benefits (FEHBP), you must leave your spouse some portion of the annuity or their health benefit will be discontinued upon your death.

*Example:* Let's assume you are either FERS or CSRS and you are nearing retirement. You need to decide how to structure your annuity with respect to survivor benefits by comparing the full Single Life annuity with the Joint & Survivor annuity. You will get a reduced lifetime annuity amount if you elect survivor benefits because it will likely need to be paid out over a longer period of time, resulting in a lower payout.

There is also another option that many people don't know about. Instead of taking the full Joint & Survivor annuity, what if you gave your spouse a very small annuity to cover expected health insurance costs and used part of the difference in cost to purchase a life insurance policy on yourself? This insurance policy would be used to replace the annuity income to the survivor in the event of your death.

For some employees (depending on age, health, and overall financial situation), it may be worth substituting enough private life insurance to provide the surviving spouse with the additional income instead of reducing or giving up a portion of the Basic or Full life annuity. We believe it is always worth reviewing your options and the costs associated with them.

Some important factors to consider are:

1. Your federal annuity Cost Of Living Adjustment.

2. Your health and age when applying for private life insurance.

3. Whether your spouse is reliant on the health benefit (FEHBP) for health insurance and whether you want (or need) to leave at least a small benefit in order for them to keep this optional benefit.

4. Whether a permanent form of life insurance may be a better choice than the increasing costs of term insurance.

An Advisor who specializes in Federal Employees and their benefits can analyze these calculations for you. It is very important to get this right, <u>because once you make the choice it cannot be changed</u>.

## Why Consider Private Life Insurance Instead of a Full Survivor Benefit?

1. A life insurance death benefit is tax-free under current law.

2. Life insurance may be a way to leave a larger benefit to your spouse or children after your death while the typical federal annuity leaves nothing to your heirs other than your spouse.

3. You can change the beneficiaries on the life insurance contract at any time and add contingent beneficiaries, if desired.

4. Life insurance may build cash value or equity in the future.

5. The cash value in a life insurance policy grows tax-deferred, without current taxation.

Three very important issues to consider:

1. These calculations impact both you and your spouse's lifetime income and should be made only when supported by a comprehensive financial plan.

2. The continuation of your surviving spouse's federal health insurance is dependent upon having at least a partial survivor annuity.

3. We strongly suggest that you seek professional tax and financial counsel before making a final decision with respect to substituting life insurance for full survivor benefits.

> *"We almost always have choices, and the better the choice, the more we will be in control of our lives."*
>
> ~William Glasser

*"It's tough to make predictions, especially about the future."*

~ Yogi Berra

# CHAPTER 8

## FEDERAL LONG TERM CARE INSURANCE PROGRAM (FLTCIP)

As most people approach retirement they begin looking ahead and contemplating their Golden Years. During this time they may ask a question that goes something like this, "What could happen financially that would disrupt my retirement?" One factor that could play a disruptive role is declining health in your later years. As a Federal Retiree, you have a comprehensive health insurance plan through the Federal Employees Health Benefits Program (FEHBP). This covers a lot of the medical expenses for hospitals and physicians, but what if you and/or your spouse's health declines to the point where constant care is needed, either at home or in a nursing home? Would your health insurance or Medicare provide the protection you need without impacting your retirement income? The answer is NO! Health insurance and Medicare are not designed to provide custodial or nursing care. So you will have to ask yourself the next question, "Do I have enough money or assets to pay for these expenses and still maintain a solid retirement strategy?"

No one likes to think about the financial impact of declining health or nursing care. In the minds of many it is the worst-case scenario, but it is difficult to argue with the statistics. About 50% of those who reach the age of 65 will need long term care at some point in their life. If you have enough income and/or assets to cover the potential cost, then you are self-insured and can plan to use your own money. If however, you do not have the assets, the declining health of you and/or your spouse could jeopardize your retirement.

If you cannot self-insure, you should consider purchasing Long Term Care insurance (LTCi) because no one likes the thought of being dependent on their children or the state for prolonged care and support.

The way we see it, LTCi is simply a risk management tool that allows you to stay independent longer by transferring some of the financial risk of needing care to an insurance company, in exchange for a premium. In that way, it works just like life or home insurance that protects against the financial risk of death or losing your home to fire.

As of this writing, John Hancock is the provider of the FLTCIP. Since the program began in 2002 there have only been two Open Seasons, one at the launch of the plan in 2002 and a second in 2011. During Open Season employees and their spouses can apply with simplified underwriting (fewer medical questions), and this can be a good time to apply if you have any health conditions that may prevent you from qualifying during regular enrollment. This simplified underwriting is also offered to new hires or recently married spouses of employees.

# FLTCIP Benefits and Costs

The Federal Plan covers a spectrum of care including care at home, adult day care, assisted living, and nursing care. There is a 90-day waiting period (or deductible) that must pass before the plan begins to pay. When choosing a long term care policy you must begin by answering these three questions:

1. How much per day do you want your policy to pay?

2. How long do you want the plan to cover you?

3. How much (if any) inflation protection do you need?

Let's look at each of the primary choices:

1. How much per day?

You may elect anywhere from $100 to $500 per day in $50 increments. So if you choose $250 per day multiplied by 365 days, your policy will potentially pay $91,250 over the course of a year. When figuring out the daily benefit needed, you should consider what long term care typically costs in your area. You should also decide if you want to insure your entire risk (cost of care) or self-insure part of the cost yourself. The higher the daily benefit amount the higher your premium, so assuming part of the risk yourself will lower your insurance cost, but increase your out-of-pocket costs.

2.  How long do you want coverage?

Coverage under the Federal Plan can be for two years, three years, five years, or your lifetime. The longer the time period for the coverage selected, the greater the premium you pay for the policy. This is because the risk to the insurance company is greater. An important factor to consider when choosing policy length is your own family history with respect to health and longevity. Have members of your family had long lives? Did they need care in their later years? How long did they need care? For example, if your parents or other close relatives lived into their eighties or later and needed care, this should weigh heavily on your decision. Does your family have a history of dementia, Alzheimer's, or other debilitating diseases in their later years? If so, you may want to choose one of the longer coverage options.

There are significant differences in cost between the different coverage periods. For example, the lifetime coverage is about twice as expensive as the three-year coverage. The two-year plan is by far the least expensive, but it is also the least likely to offer coverage for as long as you may need.

To explore all of the options, currently there is a calculator function available at www.ltcfeds.com. It is important to note that the premium rates can change in the future, and we believe that you should expect them to increase during your lifetime.

3. Do you want inflation protection, and how much?

There are two inflation protection features available within the Federal LTC Program:

A. You may elect a 4% or 5% annual compound inflation adjustment to your initial daily benefit.

B. You may elect a future purchase option, which gives you the option, every two years, to purchase an increase to your benefit based on the medical inflation index. Your premium will be adjusted (usually up) at the time your future purchase is accepted, based on your current age.

We believe it is very important to carefully consider the inflation protection options when designing your policy. Care and medical costs are increasing rapidly each year, and you will want to make sure your benefits are keeping up.

## Changes to Federal Long Term Care Coverage

As an eligible Federal Employee you are free to enroll in the program at any time. If you are currently enrolled you may reduce or increase coverage any time you wish. However, if you are increasing coverage, medical underwriting (additional questions) will apply and the coverage may or may not be accepted by the insurance company based on your current health evaluation. Also, additional costs will be assessed based on your current age and associated medical risks. This is why you should not wait until you are sick and in need of nursing care to apply to increase your long term care benefits.

**Preparing for Retirement:** Unlike the federal life and health insurance programs, your FLTCIP may be taken into retirement without a five-year coverage requirement. Retirement does not affect your LTC premiums.

Although long term care premiums are not designed to increase in the future, they can. Many early enrollees were surprised in 2011 with an increase in their FLTCIP premiums. Insurance companies also reserve the right to pass on extra underwriting costs to policyholders. In other words, if the insurance company underestimated their costs, they may pass them on to you later. Therefore, we think it very prudent to anticipate increases in these premiums during retirement.

### Federal Plan vs. Private Industry Options

When exploring your LTC options you should fully investigate both the Federal Plan and private sector policies, helping you become an educated consumer. Although offered through the government, the FLTCIP is not government insured or subsidized. The government has partnered with John Hancock Insurance Company until 2016. It is important to note that your policy in owned by you and coverage will continue as long as you pay your premiums.

Policies that are purchased through the private industry (outside the government) may offer a wider range of flexible options and features. They may also offer premium discounts for married couples or those of particularly good health as compared to the FLTCIP.

Long term care policies have several moving parts, such as variable benefit levels, inflation riders, and elimination periods, all of which can make direct comparisons difficult. Throw in trying to decide how much and which type of coverage you need and it can become quite challenging indeed.

***John and Laura's Tip***: Before you purchase long term care insurance, there are a few questions to consider:

1. Is buying coverage right for you?

2. If coverage is to be bought, which provider (the government plan or a private outside firm) and what type of policy is best?

3. Will the long term care insurance premiums be affordable through your retirement years?

Before deciding to apply for LTCi, either through FLTCIP or a private insurance company, it is important to fully understand how this decision fits into your financial and retirement plans. You need to look at the "Big Picture."

It is important to remember that you should purchase LTCi before you get sick, because the younger and healthier you are when you buy the policy, the less it will cost.

> "...if either of us needed some help, we wouldn't want to burden our children and take them away from their own families or careers to look after us."
>
> ~ Ken Dychtwald

# CHAPTER 9

## WHEN SHOULD YOU APPLY FOR SOCIAL SECURITY RETIREMENT BENEFITS?

There's a lot to consider when deciding the best time to start collecting Social Security benefits. Once people reach their 60's, they start to wonder if they should apply at 62 and grab as much money as they can, or wait until 66 or 70 to get a higher lifetime benefit.

In some respects it is a math problem. You can get a lower monthly payment for a longer period of time, or a higher payment for a shorter period of time. The decision would be much simpler if you only knew exactly how long you were going to live. While going through this analysis, Clint Eastwood might ask, "Do you feel lucky?"

If you feel lucky with respect to a long life, claiming Social Security late may seem like the best option. But in reality, longevity is only one of many factors in a complex decision. With Social Security, as well as retirement planning in general, there is no one-size-fits-all solution. Other variables to be considered include current and anticipated cash needs, other sources of retirement income, whether you plan to work after you begin benefits, and what the advantage of delaying the start of Social Security would be.

# Differences in Retirement Benefits Can be Substantial

The first step in the Social Security analysis is to find out approximately how much income you would receive at different ages. Social Security mails you an estimate once a year if you are approaching retirement age, but you can also obtain an estimate at any time from Social Security at www.socialsecurity.gov. It is simple to do and only takes a few minutes.

The following chart provides an estimate for a hypothetical worker and will illustrate how the monthly benefit can differ based on age and yearly earnings.

| Age | Monthly Benefit |
|---|---|
| 62 | $1,487 |
| 66 (full retirement) | $2,179 |
| 70 | $2,880 |

If the worker waits until full retirement age or FRA, his or her benefit will be about 47% higher than at 62 (the earliest opportunity), while waiting until age 70 nearly doubles the age 62 benefit. For each year the worker delays filing, the benefit grows by approximately 8%. It is worth noting that the Social Security retirement benefit does not grow after age 70, so there is no reason to delay benefits after that age.

## Don't Take Benefits Too Early

According to Social Security statistics, 74% of current retirees are receiving reduced benefits due to filing earlier than age 66. Your Social Security payment is based on the average of your 35 highest paid years of work, adjusted for inflation. Simply put, the longer you work, the higher your payout. The Social Security website also states that "About one out of every four 65 year olds will live past age 90." Let's think about that for a second. If you are a married couple both age 65, there is good chance that one of you will live to age 90 or beyond! So it is important to plan accordingly.

Social Security benefits continue throughout your entire life and provide valuable protection against outliving your other sources of income. So constructing a plan that gives you the best benefit over your lifetime is essential to a successful retirement.

## Complications for Married Couples

Deciding the best time to begin Social Security benefits is an even greater challenge when coordinating spousal benefits because of the rules. When analyzing Social Security options for married couples, it is important to look at different scenarios and combinations that could involve claiming benefits at different times. An example would be when one spouse claims benefits at 62 and the other at age 70.

It is important to understand that a spouse can claim the greater of Social Security benefits based on their own earnings record, **OR** they can collect a spousal benefit that will provide 50% of their spouse's benefit. However, the benefit will be less than 50% if applying before FRA. This can be helpful for spouses who never worked outside the home, or who spent a lot of time raising children, or in part-time or lower-paying positions. In such cases the spouse can collect the equivalent of half of the other spouse's benefit if it is more than the benefit based on their own earnings record.

## Divorced and Widow's Benefits

In the event of a spouse's death, widows and widowers have a survivor's benefit that can be claimed as early as age 60 (or age 50 if they are disabled). This allows them to claim up to 100% of the retirement benefit of their deceased spouse if it is higher than their own. Again, if claimed prior to your full retirement age this benefit amount will be reduced.

If you are claiming an ex-spousal benefit, were married for at least 10 years, have been divorced for at least 2 years, and have not remarried, you can claim either your own benefit or the spousal benefit, whichever is higher. If claiming before your FRA, you will get the higher amount but, you will be stuck with this amount, not being able to collect delayed credits. With delayed retirement credits, a person can receive an increased benefit of 8% for each year retirement benefits are delayed from age 66 to 70. So BE CAREFUL and know how the rules apply to you.

Other important notes regarding former spousal benefits:
- This benefit does not affect the former spouse's benefit.
- Both ex-spouses may be eligible to claim them.
- It may affect your Medicare benefit and billing.
- If you have been married and divorced more than once with the marriages lasting over 10 years, you can claim on the higher wage earner.
- Lastly, there are specific rules for claiming deceased ex-spousal benefits too.

### How Working Affects Social Security Benefits

Another aspect of Social Security planning is the opportunity to collect benefits while still working. If you are working prior to full retirement age, some of your benefits may be withheld. For 2015, the maximum amount you can earn before benefits are withheld is $15,720. For every $2 you earn over $15,720, $1 in benefits will be withheld. A special rule applies if you are receiving benefits in the year you reach full retirement age: your monthly benefit will be reduced by $1 for every $3 you earn above $41,880. After you pass full retirement age, you can continue to collect benefits without reduction no matter how much income you receive.

As you can see, the rules regarding Social Security are fairly complicated and it can be very difficult deciding the best time to apply for Social Security retirement benefits. With life expectancy extending longer than in previous generations, the timing of this decision has a significant impact on those approaching retirement age.

## Taxation of Social Security Income

When we discuss the taxation of Social Security in our federal retirement seminars, we often have people say, *"I thought Social Security was already taxed – surely they can't tax it again."* Well, sorry – they can, and they do.

The following information and calculations are from the Social Security publication "Benefits Planner: Income Taxes and Your Social Security Benefits." You can find it at http://www.ssa.gov/planners/taxes.htm:

> Some people have to pay federal income taxes on their Social Security benefits. This usually happens only if you have other substantial income (such as wages, self-employment, interest, dividends and other taxable income that must be reported on your tax return) in addition to your benefits.

> No one pays federal income tax on more than 85 percent of his or her Social Security benefits based on Internal Revenue Service (IRS) rules.

> Each January you will receive a *Social Security Benefit Statement* (form SSA-1099) showing the amount of benefits you received in the previous year. You can use this *Benefit Statement* when you complete your federal income tax return to find out if your benefits are subject to tax.

# Taxation of Social Security Benefits 2015

| Filing status | Combined Income* | Amount of SS subject to tax |
|---|---|---|
| Married filing jointly | Under $32,000 | 0 |
| | $32,000 - $44,000 | 50% |
| | Over $44,000 | 85% |
| Single, head of household, qualifying widow(er), married filing separately & living apart from spouse | Under $25,000 | 0 |
| | $25,000 - $34,000 | 50% |
| | Over $34,000 | 85% |
| Married filing separately and living with spouse | Over 0 | 85% |

**\*Combined Income:** Your adjusted gross income

+ Nontaxable interest

+ <u>50% of your Social Security benefits</u>


## What You Need to Consider Before Deciding When to Retire

For many people, deciding when to retire is one of the biggest decisions they will make in their lifetime. Social Security often plays a significant role in many people's retirement plans.

We like to think of Social Security as an inflation-protected joint and survivor annuity insured by the U.S. government. In our practice we have seen Social Security payouts provide anywhere from a very insignificant part to a major piece of a client's retirement income. The combination of several factors needs to be considered as you begin to think about retirement:

1. Life Expectancy

2. Total Retirement Assets: TSP, IRA, Other Investments

3. Health / Long Term Care Expenses

4. Expected Income Needs

5. Inflation Expectations

6. Pension Benefits

7. Tax Rates

***John and Laura's Tip***: Social Security decisions should be a part of a Comprehensive Financial Plan that addresses all of the areas of your unique financial position. We encourage everyone considering retirement to take the time to create a plan that looks at your retirement situation holistically.

# CHAPTER 10

## FOR FERS ONLY:
## THE FERS SOCIAL SECURITY SUPPLEMENT

A special benefit exists for FERS employees who retire prior to age 62 called the Special Retirement Supplement, or FERS Supplement. This benefit is surprisingly unknown by many FERS employees. The primary purpose of this benefit is to bridge the income gap of eligible FERS employees until they can begin Social Security at age 62. As we discussed before, your retirement benefits under FERS are composed like a three-legged stool (Chapter 3, page 33).

Many FERS employees have met the requirements for their MRA (Minimum Retirement Age) at 55, 56 or 57. In other words, as a FERS employee they are eligible to retire with a full Immediate Annuity/pension because they meet the necessary years of service requirements described earlier. But, if you recall in the Social Security Chapter, the minimum age to begin Social Security is 62. So, what can be done to bridge the income gap between retirement and when your Social Security begins? The FERS Supplement was designed to fill this gap until you are eligible for Social Security. This is a unique benefit not available in the private sector or to CSRS employees.

### Eligibility for the FERS Supplement

It is important to understand that **not all FERS employees are eligible** for this benefit. It is available for a normal, immediate retirement only. A deferred retirement or early retirement (MRA+10) will not qualify.

This is another way of saying that you must meet your MRA (Minimum Retirement Age) with 30 years of service, or age 60 with 20 years of service. You can also qualify for a normal immediate retirement at age 62 with five years of service, but the FERS Supplement ends at age 62 anyway, so the benefit would no longer be available.

## Estimating Your FERS Supplement

If you are considering retiring before age 62 and believe you are eligible based on the earlier discussion of the Supplement, we will provide a quick formula to estimate your benefits. For this equation you will want to have your Social Security statement and your years of service handy.

| Years of Creditable Service Divided by 40 | X | Social Security Benefit Amount at Age 62 | = | Your FERS Supplement |
|---|---|---|---|---|

This formula is an <u>estimate</u> only. If you are interested in an exact calculation please refer to the FERS handbook, Chapter 51, or call our office. Also, if you don't have your Social Security statement handy, you can estimate this by going to www.ssa.gov/estimator and following the instructions. It provides an estimate of your Social Security benefits at age 62.

*Example:* Let's say Jim, age 56, is a FERS employee and has met his MRA with 30 years of service. He has found his estimated Social Security at age 62 to be $1,200/month. Using the formula, his estimated FERS Supplement would be:

$$\underline{\textbf{30 years}} \times \textbf{\$1,200/month} = \textbf{\$900/month}$$
$$\textbf{40}$$

Jim will receive approximately 75% of his Social Security until he turns age 62, when his Supplemental benefit stops. Jim will then be eligible for his normal Social Security retirement benefit which would be the original $1,200/month.

## When the Supplement Ends at Age 62

Jim may opt <u>not</u> to take his Social Security at age 62. He may decide to wait until his full retirement at age 66, or even wait until age 70 to receive an even higher amount of the Social Security monthly retirement benefits. The longer Jim waits, the higher his benefit will be. The benefit caps at age 70, but this may create an income gap because the Supplement ends at age 62. Regardless of whether he begins collecting Social Security or waits until age 70, his FERS Supplemental benefit will stop at age 62.

It is important to understand that beginning the FERS Supplement does not impact your regular Social Security, because the FERS Supplement is funded separately by OPM. This is good news for those who are able to utilize the FERS Supplement.

# Yes, there are reductions in the FERS Supplement

The FERS Supplement is treated much like Social Security income from a taxation perspective.

While you are receiving your FERS Social Security Supplement, you are subject to the same earnings limitations as if you were taking your Social Security prior to full retirement age. With the 2015 earnings limitation at $15,720, your FERS Supplement would also be reduced by $1 for every $2 you earn above the limit. For example, if you earned $25,720, you would have earned $10,000 more than the limit. ($25,720 - $15,720 = $10,000). Therefore, your FERS Supplemental benefit would be reduced by $5,000 ($10,000/2 = $5,000) in that year.

The FERS Supplement, like Social Security, is taxable income. (Sorry about that!) The amount of tax paid depends on your combined income, which includes your adjusted gross income, non-taxable interest, plus ½ of your Social Security benefit (or Supplement) as noted on page 77.

For those filing individually, the IRS begins taxing Social Security (or Supplement) earnings at $25,000.

If you are single and have a combined income over $25,000 but below $34,000, half (50%) of your FERS Supplement is subject to federal income taxes. If you have a combined income greater than $34,000, then 85% of your Supplement will be subject to Federal income taxes.

Early Retirement Example:

Jim is single and retires at age 56. Let's assume he begins his FERS Pension annuity of $1,000/month and also elects to begin his FERS Supplement of $900/month. He also starts a part-time job earning $1,850/month. His total income reflects three sources in this example:

1. FERS Pension $12,000/year.

2. FERS Social Security Supplement $10,800/year. (Reduced by Earnings Test to $7,560*)

3. Part-time earnings $22,200/year.

Jim's estimated combined income would be the FERS Pension ($12,000) and part-time income ($22,200) and 50% of his Supplement ($3,720), which totals $37,920. At this combined income level, 85% of Jim's Social Security Supplement will be taxable income.

Also, because his earnings exceed $15,720 his Supplement will be reduced by $3,360. See the following calculation:

Earnings of $22,200 - $15,720 (earnings limit) = $6,480 excess earnings over the limit.

$6,480/$2 = $3,240** reduction in Social Security Supplement. ($10,800 - $3,240 = $7,560)

**The earnings test only applies to earned income, not pension, dividends, etc.**

**\*\*Remember the chargeback is your supplement which is reduced by \$1 for every \$2 you earn above the limit. In this case the reduction is \$3,240.**

For a full discussion of this topic, please see Social Security PUB No. 05-10069 "How Work Affects Your Benefits," located at: www.socialsecurity.gov/pubs/EN-05-10069.pdf.

### Are You Planning to Retire Before Age 62?

If you are planning to retire before age 62, you will need to calculate your FERS Supplement and the possible reductions and taxes associated with it. The FERS Supplement may be a useful benefit to make an early retirement possible. However, a "Big Picture" analysis, looking at all three legs of the retirement stool (including your spouse's income, if applicable) is important because of the integration and complexity of the benefits and respective taxes.

# CHAPTER 11

## SOCIAL SECURITY PLANNING AND THE CSRS EMPLOYEE

As a CSRS employee, one of the primary benefits offered to you by the government is your retirement annuity. This annuity benefit is very favorable because it offers a high payout, annual Cost Of Living Adjustments, and flexible payments to your survivor. On the negative side, it does limit both your Social Security income and spousal benefits.

### Windfall Elimination Provision (WEP)

In 1986 Congress passed the Windfall Elimination Provision (WEP). The general idea behind the WEP is to prevent CSRS, CSRS Offset, and FERS Transfers from double dipping in both the CSRS Annuity and full Social Security payments.

The general rules regarding qualification for Social Security are that you need a minimum of 40 quarters (or 10 years) of non-government work to qualify for any retirement benefits. However, Congress specified that CSRS Annuity qualifiers must have both the 40 quarters AND an additional 30 years of Substantial Earnings under Social Security to qualify for full benefits, otherwise it will be reduced. What constitutes Substantial Earnings? They are the minimum earnings needed in a particular year to receive Social Security credit for that year.

## Substantial Earnings Chart

| | | | | | | | |
|---|---|---|---|---|---|---|---|
| 1937-54 | $900 | 1980 | $5,100 | 1993 | $10,725 | 2006 | $17,475 |
| 1955-58 | $1,050 | 1981 | $5,550 | 1994 | $11,250 | 2007 | $18,150 |
| 1959-65 | $1,200 | 1982 | $6,075 | 1995 | $11,325 | 2008 | $18,975 |
| 1966-67 | $1,650 | 1983 | $6,675 | 1996 | $11,625 | 2009 | $19,800 |
| 1968-71 | $1,950 | 1984 | $7,050 | 1997 | $12,150 | 2010 | $19,800 |
| 1972 | $2,250 | 1985 | $7,425 | 1998 | $12,675 | 2011 | $19,800 |
| 1973 | $2,700 | 1986 | $7,875 | 1999 | $13,425 | 2012 | $20,475 |
| 1974 | $3,300 | 1987 | $8,175 | 2000 | $14,175 | 2013 | $21,075 |
| 1975 | $3,525 | 1988 | $8,400 | 2001 | $14,925 | 2014 | $21,750 |
| 1976 | $3,824 | 1989 | $8,925 | 2002 | $15,750 | 2015 | $22,050 |
| 1977 | $4,125 | 1990 | $9,525 | 2003 | $16,125 | | |
| 1978 | $4,425 | 1991 | $9,900 | 2004 | $16,275 | | |
| 1979 | $4,725 | 1992 | $10,300 | 2005 | $16,725 | | |

If you do not qualify with 30 years of Substantial Earnings (listed above), the Windfall Elimination Provision (WEP) will limit your Social Security benefit. You will lose 5% of your PIA (Primary Insurance Amount - the basic Social Security benefit based on career earnings) for every year of Substantial Earnings below 30, but the government does cap the benefit reduction. No greater than a 60% total reduction is possible. Stated differently, you can receive no less than 40% of Social Security benefits as shown in the following chart.

| Years of Substantial Earnings | Percentage |
|---|---|
| 30 or more | 90% |
| 29 | 85% |
| 28 | 80% |
| 27 | 75% |
| 26 | 70% |
| 25 | 65% |
| 24 | 60% |
| 23 | 55% |
| 22 | 50% |
| 21 | 45% |
| 20 or less | 40% |

For more information, see "Windfall Elimination Provision" (PUB No. 05-10045), found on the Social Security website: http://www.socialsecurity.gov/pubs/EN-05-10045.pdf.

***John and Laura's Tip***: Remember, the Social Security statements that you and your spouse receive annually do not take into account the WEP or GPO (Government Pension Offset).

## Government Pension Offset (GPO)

The general idea behind the GPO is to prevent CSRS annuitants from collecting both their CSRS Annuity and the Social Security benefits of a current or former spouse.

Under the general Social Security rules, a worker is entitled to get 100% of his or her Social Security benefit or 50% of a living spouse or ex-spouse's Social Security benefit, whichever is greater, but not both. This is called a spousal benefit.

As a result of the WEP, a CSRS annuitant may have their own Social Security reduced below their spousal benefit amount from a current or former spouse. To prevent a CSRS annuitant from benefiting from what they call an Unearned Social Security Benefit, the government introduced the GPO or Government Pension Offset.

If the GPO applies, your Social Security spousal benefit will be reduced by 2/3 of your government pension, <u>and could be reduced all the way to zero</u>. To learn more, see Government Pension Offset (PUB No. 05-10007), found at http://www.socialsecurity.gov/pubs/EN-05-10007.pdf.

***<u>John and Laura's Tip</u>***: If you are a CSRS employee and the GPO applies thus reducing your spouse and widow's benefit, it may be beneficial to have your spouse take their Social Security retirement benefits early (at 62), because the typical Social Security survivor benefits will be reduced. Since you are CSRS, several factors must be examined before making this decision, such as income needs and life expectancy. Don't forget about the Social Security earnings test! (Chapter 11, page 83)

Also, don't be afraid to get professional help. Once these deductions are made most of them are irrevocable!

# CHAPTER 12

## FEHBP AND MEDICARE: HOW THEY WORK TOGETHER FOR FEDERAL RETIREES

The cost of health insurance is one of the largest expenses Federal Employees will have to pay in their retirement years. As you plan for your retirement, we recommend that you carefully examine how the Federal Employee Health Benefits Plan (FEHBP) and Medicare work together in your unique situation.

While FEHBP and Medicare generally complement each other, there can be gaps in coverage, particularly for custodial nursing home care. (As we noted in Chapter 8, neither form of health insurance is intended to cover long term custodial care).

Generally speaking, Medicare is the primary coverage for annuitants (and spouses who are covered under a self and family enrollment) who are age 65 or older. In this case, FEHBP becomes the secondary insurance.

For Federal Employees who continue to work beyond age 65 (and who are enrolled in FEHBP), FEHBP continues to be their primary coverage and Medicare is the secondary coverage.

# Medicare Basics

Medicare is a health insurance program for:

1. People who are 65 years of age and older.

2. Some people with disabilities who are less than 65 years of age.

3. People with End-Stage Renal Disease (ESRD - permanent kidney failure requiring dialysis or a transplant).

Medicare has four primary parts:

**Part A (hospital insurance):** Most people do not have to pay for Part A. If you or your spouse worked for at least 10 years in Medicare-covered employment, you should be able to qualify for premium-free Part A insurance (anyone who was a Federal Employee on January 1, 1983 automatically qualifies). Otherwise, if you are age 65 or older, you may be able to buy it. Contact 1-800-MEDICARE for more information.

**Part B (medical insurance):** Most people pay a monthly premium for Part B. These premiums are withheld from your monthly Social Security check or your retirement check.

**Part C (Medicare Advantage):** If you are eligible for Medicare, you may have options for how you get your health care.

Medicare Advantage is the term used to describe the various managed health plan options available to Medicare participants. You must be enrolled in Medicare parts A and B to join a Medicare Advantage Plan. These are health care choices (like HMOs) available in some areas of the country. In most Medicare managed care plans, you can only go to doctors, specialists, or hospitals that are within the plan. Medicare managed care plans provide all the benefits that basic Medicare covers. Some cover extras, like prescription drugs. To learn more about enrolling in a Medicare managed care plan, contact Medicare at 1-800-MEDICARE (1-800-633-4227) or at www.medicare.gov.

**Part D (Medicare prescription drug coverage).** There is a monthly premium for Part D coverage. Most Federal Employees do not need to enroll in the Medicare drug program, since all FEHBPs will have prescription drug benefits that are at least equal to the standard Medicare prescription drug coverage. Still, you may want to be aware of the benefits Medicare is offering.

***John and Laura's Tip:*** It will generally be to your advantage to keep your current FEHBP drug coverage without any changes. An exception may be for those with limited incomes who may qualify for Medicare's extra help with prescription drug costs. We suggest that you contact your benefits administrator or your FEHBP insurer for information about your FEHBP coverage before making any coverage changes.

## Should Federal Employees Enroll in Medicare Part A?

The decision to enroll in Medicare is yours. We encourage you to apply for Medicare benefits three months before you turn 65. It's an easy process. Just call the Social Security Administration toll-free number (1-800-772-1213) and set up an appointment to apply. If you do not apply for one or more parts of Medicare, you can still be covered under the FEHBP.

***John and Laura's Tip***: If you can get premium-free Part A coverage, we advise you to enroll in it, <u>even if you are still working</u>. Most Federal Employees and annuitants are entitled to Medicare Part A at age 65 **without cost**. When you don't have to pay premiums for Medicare Part A, it makes good sense to obtain coverage. It can reduce your out-of-pocket expenses such as deductibles, coinsurance and charges that exceed your plan's allowable charges. Medicare also covers particular medical expenses, which some FEHBPs may not cover or only partially cover (check your plan brochure for details).

## As a Federal Retiree Do You Need to Enroll in Medicare Part B?

Retired Federal Employees are entitled to Medicare under the same rules as all other retirees. You are first eligible to enroll in Part B during your initial enrollment period, which begins three months before you turn 65 and ends three months after you turn 65. If you do not enroll in Part B during your initial enrollment period, you may only enroll during the General Enrollment Period, which is from January 1<sup>st</sup> through March

31$^{st}$ each year. Part B coverage is effective July 1$^{st}$ of the year of enrollment. If you did not enroll when you were first eligible, you may have to pay higher Part B premiums. Your Part B monthly premium can go up 10% for each 12 month period that you could have had Part B, but didn't sign up for it.

The Social Security Administration handles Medicare eligibility and enrollment. To sign up for Medicare or to add Medicare Part B, call Social Security.

You don't have to take Part B coverage if you don't want it, and your FEHBP can't require you to take it. However, there are some advantages to enrolling in Part B:

1. You have the advantage of coordination of benefits between Medicare and your FEHBP, reducing your out-of-pocket costs.

2. You must be enrolled in Parts A and B to join a Medicare Advantage plan.

3. Your FEHBP may waive its copayments, coinsurance, and deductibles for Part B services.

4. Some services covered under Part B might not be covered or only partially covered by your plan. This includes orthopedic and prosthetic devices, and some medical equipment and home health care.

5. If you are enrolled in an FEHBP HMO, and Medicare is the primary payer, you may go outside of the plan's network for Part B services and receive reimbursement by Medicare. Check your FEHBP brochure for details.

It is important to understand that the FEHBP contracts are renewed each year, so your current plan's coverage, cost, or benefits may change next year. FEHBP can also terminate their contract with the Office of Personnel Management. You should take this into consideration when deciding whether to enroll in Part B. The Office of Personnel Management provides useful information to retiring Federal Employees at http://www.opm.gov/insure/health/eligibility/annuitants.asp. To add Medicare Part B, you should contact the Social Security Administration.

### How Much Does Part B Coverage Cost?

Everyone is charged a premium for Medicare Part B coverage. The premium amount is available in the "Medicare & You" handbook produced by the U.S. Centers for Medicare and Medicaid (CMS) and is also available on the Medicare website at www.medicare.gov.

Most people will pay $104.90 per month in 2015. However, the premiums vary according to your yearly income and are subject to annual adjustments. We suggest that you review the information and decide if it makes sense to buy the Medicare Part B coverage for your situation.

## _John and Laura's Tip:_

Your FEHBP carrier brochure is available at:
http://www.opm.gov/healthcare-insurance/healthcare/plan-information/.

It explains how benefits are coordinated with Medicare, depending on the type of Medicare managed care plan you have. If you are eligible for Medicare coverage, you should read this information carefully, as it will have a significant bearing on your benefits.

We suggest that you take the time to educate yourself or to seek out a consultant familiar with both the FEHBP and Medicare for assistance.

"As we express our gratitude, we must never forget that the highest appreciation is not to utter words, but to live by them."

~ John F. Kennedy

*"Nothing is impossible,*

*the word itself says,*

*'I'm Possible'!"*

~ Audrey Hepburn

# CHAPTER 13

## VOLUNTARY CONTRIBUTION PROGRAM (VCP)

The Voluntary Contribution Plan is available to CSRS employees and can significantly increase their retirement savings by allowing them to contribute up to 10% of their lifetime federal earnings to this account. Unfortunately, FERS employees and those who chose to transfer to FERS from CSRS are not eligible to contribute to the Voluntary Contribution Program.

Many CSRS employees are unaware of the VCP and its benefits, even though the program has been in existence since 1939. It is simply not advertised and has become a generally unknown secret!

The VCP was created to allow CSRS and CSRS Offset participants to supplement their annuity at retirement by contributing after-tax dollars up to 10% of their basic salary. If you study the details of the program, you will note that contributions can be made retroactively, back to the date of hire. You must be an active employee to contribute to the VCP; retirees are not eligible. Also, if you owe a deposit or redeposit, you are required to pay off the deposit before being able to contribute to the VCP account. Again, the contributions can only be made with after-tax contributions, so an eligible employee must have additional money set aside to contribute to the plan. These funds can come from your personal savings and investments or from inherited monies. The interest earned on the deposit is tax-deferred as long as it remains in the account.

The VCP also offers a lot of flexibility. You can contribute to your VCP a little at a time or with one big check prior to retirement. Deposits must be made in increments of $25. CSRS participants may withdraw their contributions at any time, for any reason before retirement. As we stated before, there would be no tax on the contributions because of the after-tax nature of the account. However, the interest is not tax-free and it would need to be transferred to a Traditional IRA to avoid taxation. Otherwise there may be a 10% early withdrawal penalty tax on that interest if you are under the age of 59½.

## VCP Annuity Option

At retirement, voluntary contributions, with interest, may be used in several ways. One choice is to purchase an additional annuity. This will be added to the regular CSRS Annuity, which is unaffected by the VCP Annuity. These two annuities are mutually exclusive, so when you annuitize your VCP you are trading the entire balance for a fixed stream of income over your lifetime.

The rules regarding the VCP Annuity have some similarities and some very significant differences to your CSRS Annuity.

Similarities:

1. The VCP Annuity is for life, similar to the regular CSRS Annuity.

2. You may elect a survivor option for a spouse just like the CSRS Annuity.

## Differences:

1. There is no COLA (Cost of Living Adjustment) with the VCP Annuity.

2. The internal calculation of the VCP Annuity income payout is different: Each $100 deposited in the account will provide an annuity payment of $7 a year for life at age 55, increasing 20 cents per year for each year the annuitant is over 55 at the starting point of the income. Thus, if you retire at age 60, each $100 will buy $8 a year of the VCP life annuity; at age 62, $8.40 a year; and so forth.

3. With the VCP, you can elect a survivor benefit for a spouse, a child, or any person, related or unrelated to you. This can be the same person designated on your regular CSRS Annuity or a different person entirely. If you elect a survivor benefit, your annuity will be reduced and your survivor will be paid half of the annuity for their life. The calculation of the original annuity amount depends on the difference in age between the annuitant and the survivor. For example, a younger survivor annuitant will have a greater payout reduction.

The Voluntary Contribution Election form #**RI 38-124** can be used to elect a VCP Annuity.

## Buying the VCP Annuity

The more money you have in your VCP and the longer you wait to buy an annuity, the higher your income payments will be. Why? Annuities are calculated based on your age. The older you are, the shorter the life expectancy calculation, therefore the less time the insurance company will be paying you income.

***John and Laura's Tip:*** If you are thinking about electing an annuity and the guaranteed income it provides, you should explore your options in the private market first, because it is quite possible that you may be able to do better than the standard VCP Annuity in terms of the monthly income provided.

## Roth Conversion Opportunity

Something to consider: A very unique opportunity exists for CSRS employees to enhance their retirement savings with the use of the VCP. As we have already explained, the participation rules state that eligible employees may contribute up to 10% of their lifetime earnings. This can be done retroactively any time before they retire. According to IRS notification 2008-30, the after-tax portion of the VCP can then be rolled into a Roth IRA. This is true even if the employee's salary level would normally make them ineligible to contribute to a Roth IRA.

**It is important to understand the significance of the above information.** This is a way for CSRS employees to transfer up to 10% of their career earnings into a Roth IRA. Wow! This means that any income generated from your Roth will be tax-free for the remainder of your life and the lives of your beneficiaries too! It is important to understand that the general rules of a Roth IRA (discussed later in the chapter) must be followed.

Roth Conversion Hypothetical Example: Jim is 60 and is a CSRS employee nearing retirement. Over the course of his career he has earned $2,000,000. Jim was able to save $200,000 which he has in a savings account at his local bank. Before he retires, Jim could open a VCP account and deposit the entire $200,000 (10% of his lifetime earnings) into the account. This account would immediately begin to earn tax-deferred interest (recently 1.625%). Jim could choose to wait until retirement and begin his VCP Annuity. Since Jim is 60 and has deposited $200,000 into the account, his life annuity would be $200,000 divided by 100, or $2,000. If you recall, every $100 invested in the VCP will purchase $8 a year of the VCP Annuity at age 60. So 2000 times the factor $8 would equal a lifetime income of $16,000 annually. If Jim elected a survivor, it would lower his income amount depending on the age of the person he chose.

If Jim decides the annuity option is not a good alternative for him, his second option is to establish a Roth IRA and transfer the entire balance into the new account. This is permitted even though Jim would typically not be able to deposit money into a Roth IRA because of the Roth contribution limits and eligibility rules. Once the funds are in the Roth IRA, Jim can invest the money as he desires. When Jim decides to make withdrawals from his Roth IRA, the income he withdraws will remain tax-free as long as Jim follows the Roth

IRA regulations. Additionally, any remainder will transfer tax-free to his beneficiaries.

## Roth IRA Basics

With a Roth IRA, you pay taxes before the money is contributed into the account. Because the taxes are paid in advance, no taxes are paid on withdrawals from the account. This is different from a Traditional IRA that allows you to defer taxes now and pay taxes later on withdrawals from the account. With a Traditional IRA you will typically get a deduction from your taxable income in the year you contribute funds, but you will not with a Roth IRA.

The Roth can be greatly beneficial when the money is allowed to grow for many years before it is withdrawn tax-free. Just like Traditional IRAs, the Roth has restrictions to access the funds. The money must remain in the account for a minimum of five years and until you reach 59½. If these rules are followed you can withdraw the principal and earnings tax-free. If these rules are not followed and withdrawals are made before five years, a 10% penalty plus income tax must be paid on the earnings. Please refer to IRS PUB No. 590 "Individual Retirement Arrangements" for more specific details.

# A Final Word on Roth IRAs

We believe the Roth IRA is a wonderful opportunity to enjoy tax-free income/withdrawals to supplement your CSRS Annuity during retirement. This is particularly important if you believe (as we do) that tax rates are likely to increase in the future.

# Getting Started

***John and Laura's Tip***: If you are seriously considering taking advantage of this special opportunity for CSRS employees, it is a good idea to get the advice of a Financial Advisor familiar with the VCP program.

Here is how to establish an account:

1. Submit form **SF 2804** to your agency retirement benefits office. Do not send a check yet. We recommend that you establish your account at least a few months in advance of retirement. However, you may submit the form with your retirement application.

2. OPM will send you notification that the account has been established and is ready to accept your Voluntary Contribution check.

3. Mail your personal check in the amount of your desired contribution. Remember that this may not exceed 10% of your total career earnings. Additional checks can be deposited while working in increments of $25.

If you establish the account as you are retiring, you will only have the one opportunity to make a deposit.

4. If you decide to withdraw your VCP and transfer it to a Roth IRA, you will need to submit form **RI 38-124**. Instructions are on form **RI 38-125**.
   *You may also withdraw your contributions without utilizing the Roth with the same forms.

5. It is **very important** to file your Voluntary Contributions withdrawal request prior to finalizing your retirement with OPM. <u>A refund or rollover must be requested in order to take advantage of the Roth IRA option</u>. If you do not, the claims examiner will process your contributions as an additional annuity and add it to your CSRS retirement! Few people desire this option.

***John and Laura's Tip:*** It is possible that the benefits specialist in your agency may not be familiar with the program because only a few employees set up the Voluntary Contribution account. If this is the case, please refer them to Chapter 31 of the CSRS and FERS handbook.

# Let's Summarize the VCP Benefits

Up to 10% of your career lifetime earnings can be contributed into the plan retroactively before retirement.

The VCP can be used to create additional guaranteed income with the VCP annuity option at retirement.

The VCP offers the flexibility to withdraw the funds (for any reason) prior to, or at retirement.

With the VCP, you have the ability to transfer the after-tax contributions to a Roth IRA.

The current yield is 1.625% (2013), which is attractive given the current low interest rate environment.

The flexibility of the VCP combined with the ability to convert deposits to a Roth IRA is a unique benefit that should not be overlooked.

# Recent Voluntary Contribution Rates of Return

1995.................................................................7.0%

1996.................................................................6.875%

1997.................................................................6.875%

1998.................................................................6.75%

1999.................................................................5.75%

2000.................................................................6.375%

2001.................................................................6.375%

2002.................................................................5.5%

2003.................................................................5.0%

2004.................................................................3.875%

2005.................................................................4.375%

2006.................................................................4.125%

2007.................................................................4.875%

2008.................................................................4.75%

2009.................................................................3.875%

2010.................................................................3.125%

2011.................................................................2.75%

2012.................................................................2.25%

2013.................................................................1.625%

# CHAPTER 14

## DOCUMENTS YOU WILL NEED TO HAVE WHEN PREPARING TO RETIRE FROM FEDERAL SERVICE

When you are thinking about retirement, it would be very helpful to establish a file called "Important Retirement Documents." These forms should be printed out as they will be needed for verification and to begin accurate benefit amounts. It is up to you to verify their accuracy, so if mistakes have been made along the way, you should correct them before you are ready to retire.

### Official Personnel Folder (OPF)

Your OPF contains the primary administrative documents used by the government to make accurate decisions throughout a Federal Employee's career. This file will verify and show validity of your federal employment. A copy of your OPF can be obtained by contacting your human resource office. It includes:

1. **SF 50** - "Notification of Personnel Action." This form is to establish and reinstate federal employment. This form also lists grades, occupation, and pay. All of your career SF 50 forms should be in your OPF.

2. **DD 214** - "Certificate of Release or Discharge from Active Duty." This is a document of the United States Department of Defense, issued upon a military service

member's retirement, separation or discharge from active-duty military service. You may be able to count military time towards federal service. This will depend on when the service occurred and if a deposit for retirement was made.

3. Records regarding choices under your federal benefits programs:

   A. Health Benefits Registration

   B. **SF 1153** - "Designation of Beneficiary under FEGLI." (the Federal Employee Group Life Insurance program). It is important to check this form every three to five years to make sure your listed beneficiaries reflect your current wishes.

   C. **SF 2808** - "Designation of Beneficiary Civil Service Program." This form designates who will receive your contribution to the retirement system if you pass away before you receive the contributions back through benefits. This form was completed when you first began service. Again, you should review to make sure your beneficiaries are accurate and the form is up-to-date.

D. **TSP-3** - "Designation of TSP Beneficiary." This form designates who will inherit your Thrift Savings Plan if you pass away. You should verify that this form is correct and up-to-date.

4. Certified copies of Birth Certificates for you and your spouse. When applying for Medicare and Social Security you will need to verify your age. Your birth certificate(s) may also be needed if a mistake is found on other documents. Also, it may be necessary to verify your spouse's date of birth if survivorship options are selected.

5. A copy of your Social Security statement. This statement shows how many years you have worked under Social Security and an estimate of your benefits. It is wise to review your Social Security earnings each year because mistakes can and do happen. It is up to you to identify them and get them corrected. Social Security gives you three years to discover any errors and have them corrected. In the course of our careers we have seen entire years of earnings not credited on Social Security statements for this reason. If an error is found, you should schedule an appointment at your local Social Security office to begin the correction process. Social Security has once again begun to mail statements to those approaching retirement age. If you have not received a recent mailing, you can go online at

www.ssa.gov and view or print your estimated benefits. You can also request a full earnings statement by year so that you can review it for accuracy.

6. A copy of your marriage license (if applicable). This will be needed when you submit your retirement paperwork to OPM. They will want to verify that you are married and your survivor benefits are legitimate.

***John and Laura's Tip***: It is important to consolidate and carefully review your personnel records and other associated personal documents and statements prior to beginning the actual retirement process. Having them organized and in good order prior to submitting your retirement paperwork can prevent headaches and possible delays.

> "In football, like in life, you must learn to play within the rules of the game."
>
> ~ Hayden Fry

# CHAPTER 15

## THE BEST DAY TO RETIRE FOR FEDERAL
## EMPLOYEES

There are many factors involved in deciding whether you are prepared and eligible to retire from federal service. In this chapter, we will assume that you have gone through the process of deciding that you are financially prepared and are trying to choose which day to walk out the door. So, with that in mind, let's look at some of things you need to consider.

> "The best time to start thinking about your
>
> retirement is before the boss does."
>
> ~ Author Unknown

### Annual Leave

One of the benefits your exit date affects is the lump sum annual (use-it or lose-it) leave payment. Employees are permitted to carry over a maximum of 240 hours (30 days) of annual leave from one year to the next. In your final year of work, you can also take unused leave from that final year as a lump sum payment.

Let's say you do carry over the maximum 240 hours into your final year. Additionally, let's say you earn 8 hours of annual leave per pay period, or 200 hours for the entire year. If you don't use any of your leave during the year, you will have a total of 440 hours of annual leave paid to you in a lump sum when you retire.

For this reason, the majority of Federal Employees choose to retire at the end of the year because it combines the end of a pay period and the end of the annual leave year, maximizing the lump sum annual leave payment. Also, if you retire at the end of the calendar year, the lump sum will be paid out in the new year and apply toward the following year's tax return, when your taxable income may be at a lower tax rate if your retired pay is lower (as with most retirees).

If a COLA (Cost of Living Adjustment) is announced in your final year, you will receive the increase on your leave as well. The lump sum will by and large be paid within two to three months after you separate. Also, taxes will generally be withheld at a higher than normal rate. The extra taxes that are withheld (if any) will be paid back when you file your next year's tax return. No other typical expenses, such as retirement contributions, TSP contributions, or insurance premiums are withheld from your lump sum.

## CSRS Employee Annuity Considerations

An employee under the CSRS system may retire on the first, second or the third day of the month and still receive credit for that month in the annuity calculator. When a CSRS employee retires after the third of the month, credit will begin on the first day of the following month. Incidentally, if you retire on the last day of the month, you can avoid unpaid days because you will begin credit on the first of the next month. Following are some examples.

**Example One:**

CSRS employee, Joe, retires September 4, 2015. His first payment for the month of October can be expected around November 1, 2015. No credit will be given for the month of September 2015 because he was not off the payroll system by the 3$^{rd}$ of the month. As stated above, the current month's credit will be given only if you retire on the first, second, or third of the month. Therefore, the third of the month is often the chosen day for CSRS retirees.

**Example Two:**

CSRS employee, Jane, retires on June 30, 2015. She can expect her first annuity check around August 1, 2015. The first check will be for the entire month of July.

**Example Three:**

CSRS employee, Fritz, retires January 3, 2015. He can expect his first pension check around February 1$^{st}$, which will cover the dates January 4$^{th}$ – January 31$^{st}$, which is the prorata portion of the month. In addition, he will be paid his salary (which is usually higher than his pension) through the third, with the first annuity check starting on the fourth. Finally, if the third is also the end of the pay period, he will accrue 8 hours of additional annual leave plus 4 hours of additional sick leave.

***John and Laura's Tips for CSRS retirees:*** Taking into account the annuity and annual leave, as well as taxation considerations discussed thus far, we believe the best day for a CSRS employee to retire is usually January 3$^{rd}$. The next best day is usually the 3$^{rd}$ of any other month.

## The FERS Employee Annuity Considerations

The FERS rules are different than the CSRS. This retirement system <u>requires</u> a break in employment for one month in order to receive credit for that month.

**Example One:** Jim decided to retire on November 30, 2015. His first annuity check will be for the month of December 2015 and should be received around January 1, 2016.

**Example Two:** Sue decides to retire on November 3, 2015. Her first check will still be received on or near January 1, 2016, representing the month of December 2015. However, no credit will be given for November because you must have the full one-month break in service to receive credit for your last month. By not leaving on the last day of the month, Sue will have 19 unpaid days before her annuity begins.

***John and Laura's Tips for FERS retirees:*** For a FERS employee, we believe retiring on the last day of the month allows you to maximize your benefits. Since you are paid through the last day of the month, you will eliminate unpaid days before your annuity begins in 30 days. If you combine the last day of the month with the end of a pay period, you will accrue the most sick and annual leave for that pay period.

Taking into account the FERS Annuity, annual leave and tax considerations, we believe for many FERS employees that the best day to retire is on December 31st. However, if you have a large annual leave balance, you may want to consider the "end of annual leave date." For 2015 it is January 9, 2016. However, you must crunch the numbers to find your personal "best" retirement date and find out if it pays off or not.

Are you confused yet? This can be complicated!

Important Note Regarding Sick Leave: Beginning January 1, 2014, sick leave increased to a full (100%) credit towards the FERS Annuity calculation.

> *"Failure occurs because of two reasons:*
>
> *Doing things without thinking about them.*
>
> *Thinking about things without doing them."*
>
> ~ Anonymous

*"I'm retired –*

*Good Bye tension,*

*HELLO Pension!"*

~ Author Unknown

# Final Thoughts

We hope that you found this book to be an understandable and valuable tool to help you on your walk to retirement. Please feel free to pass this resource on to any friends or colleagues whom you think may benefit from it as well.

If you have any comments or suggestions on how it can be improved for the next edition, we would love to hear your thoughts (positive or negative). You can reach us at 301-990-9704.

For any questions or concerns that we did not either fully address or about which you would like a further explanation, we welcome the opportunity to assist you and provide you with the information and tools you need to ensure that your retirement goals and dreams are in sight.

We would like to thank God for all the blessings he has given us – including but not limited to – our business partners for their personal and professional support; our staff, for their hard work and dedication; and our clients, who continue to trust us to help them navigate their financial goals.

Sincerely,

*John and Laura Stohlman*

Enter His gates with thanksgiving and His courts with praise; give thanks to Him and praise His name.

Psalm 100:4

# APPENDIX 1

## USEFUL FEDERAL CONTACTS

**Office of Personnel Management (OPM)**

➢ See OPM Online Services for information on what you can do at: www.opm.gov

➢ Retiree/Annuitant Information (Have your CSA or CSF retirement claim number at hand when you contact OPM):
Phone: 888-767-6738
In the Washington, DC area call: 202-606-0500
TTY: 800-878-5707
Email: retire@opm.gov

Write: OPM Retirement Operations center
P O Box 45
Boyers, PA 16017-0045

➢ OPM pamphlets, publications and forms:
www.opm.gov Click on "Forms" at the top of the page.

**Federal Employees Health Benefits Program (FEHBP)**

➢ Website: www.opm.gov/insure
Federal Employees Health Care Fraud Hotline:
Email: OIGHotline@opm.gov
Phone: 202-418-3300

## Federal Employee Group Life Insurance (FEGLI)

> ➤ Current Federal Employees must contact their human resources office. OPM and the Office of Federal Employee Group Life Insurance do not have access to your records.

> ➤ Federal retirees must contact the OPM Retirement Office at 888-767-6738 or send an email to fegli@opm.gov

> ➤ To calculate premiums, go to: www.opm.gov/calculator/worksheet.asp

> ➤ To download forms, go to: www.opm.gov/insure/life/fegli/index.asp

## Federal Employee Dental and Vision Insurance Program (FEDVIP)

> ➤ Visit the official enrollment site for FEDVIP at www.benefeds.com or call 877-888-3337 if you have any changes or comments related to your FEDVIP coverage.
> Website: www.opm.gov/insure

## Federal Long Term Care Insurance Program (FLTCIP)

> ➤ Contact Long Term Care Partners, administrator of the program:
> 800-582-3337
> TTY: 800-843-3557
> Email: Ltc@opm.gov

## Federal Flexible Spending Account Program (FSAFEDS)

> ➤ Phone: 877-372-3337
> TTY: 800-952-0450
> Website: www.fsafeds.com

**Social Security Administration (SSA)**

➤ Have your Social Security number or claim number at hand when you contact the SSA:
Phone: 800-772-1213
TTY: 800-325-0778

➤ You can apply for Social Security benefits and Medicare benefits online at www.ssa.gov. You may, however, want to make an appointment with your local Social Security office to sign up for Medicare, particularly if you want the premiums deducted from your federal retirement annuity.

➤ Write: Social Security Administration
Office of Public Inquiries
Windsor Park Building
6401 Security Blvd.
Baltimore, MD 21235

**Medicare**

➤ To make an appointment with your local Social Security office regarding signing up for Medicare, call 800-772-1213.

➤ To sign up online, go to www.ssa.gov/medicareonly

➤ To track Medicare claim status, etc., online, go to:
www.MyMedicare.gov

**Thrift Savings Plan**

➤ Phone: 877-968-3778
TTY: 877-847-4385
Website: www.tsp.gov

➤ Write: Thrift Savings Plan
P. O. Box 385021
Birmingham, AL 35238

**Internal Revenue Service**

- Phone: 800-829-1040
  TTY: 800-829-4059

- For IRS publications, call 800-829-3676
  forms and publications also can be downloaded from the IRS website at www.irs.gov

**Department of Veterans Affairs**

- VA benefits: 800-827-1000
  TTY: 800-829-4833
  Beneficiaries receiving pension benefits: 877-294-6380
  VA health care benefits: 877-222-8387
  Veterans Group Life Insurance Program: 800-419-1473
  All other VA life insurance: 800-669-8477
  Website: www.va.gov

**National Personnel Records Center (NPRC)**

- 1 Archives Drive
  St. Louis, MO 63138
  314-801-0800
  MPR.center@nara.gov

# APPENDIX 2

## DESIGNATION/RECOGNITION LIST

**CFP**®            Certified Financial Planner™ practitioner
                   www.cfp.net
                   800-322-4237

**ChFC**®           Chartered Financial Consultant
                   www.theamericancollege.edu
                   888-263-7265

**ChFEBC** ℠        Chartered Federal Employee Benefits Consultant
                   www.fedseminars.com
                   800-696-3505

**CEP**®            Chartered Estate Planner
                   National Institute of Certified Estate Planners
                   www.nicep.org
                   765-453-4300

**CLU**®            Chartered Life Underwriter
                   www.theamericancollege.edu
                   888-263-7265

**CSA**             Certified Senior Advisor
                   www.csa.us
                   800-653-1785

**RFC**             Registered Financial Consultant
                   www.iarfc.org
                   800-532-9060

**MDRT-TOT**        Million Dollar Round Table's Top of the Table
                   www.mdrt.org
                   847-692-6378